DUAL DISORDERS RECOVERY COUNSELING

A Biopsychosocial Treatment Model for Addiction and Psychiatric Illness

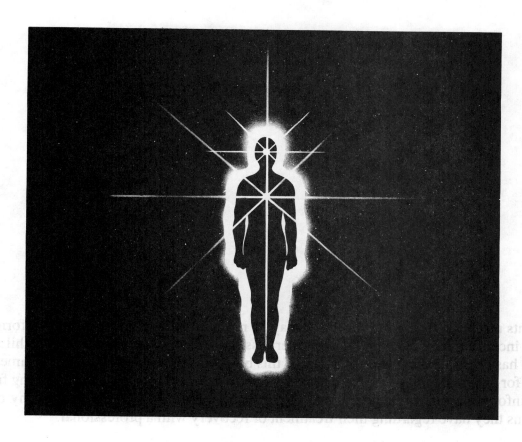

By

Dennis C. Daley, M.S.W.
and
Michael E. Thase, M.D.

Foreword by Terence T. Gorski

Herald House / Independence Press
Independence, Missouri

Additional copies of this book are available from the publisher:
    Herald House/Independence Press
    3225 South Noland Road
    P.O. Box 1770
    Independence, MO 64055-0770
    Phone: 1-800-767-8181 or 816/252-5010

Table of Contents

Foreword

Many chemically dependent people are suffering from dual diagnosis that includes both chemical dependency and related mental or personality disorders. These dual disorders are serious because they can lead to relapse if they are not properly treated.

For many years I have believed that there needs to be a comprehensive guideline for dealing with dual disorder patients in group therapy. When I became familiar with Dennis Daley's work in the dual disorder field I was impressed. I had the privilege of presenting with him at a NIDA panel of experts and asked him if he would be interested in publishing an expanded version of his model complete with session-by-session breakdowns of his group protocol. I was delighted when he agreed because his work is concrete, specific, and field-tested over a number of years with dual disorder patients.

I was also delighted that he invited Michael Thase, M.D., to coauthor this treatment manual for clinicians. Dr. Thase is a highly regarded expert in the treatment of psychiatric disorders and has considerable expertise in both pharmacotherapy and cognitive therapy of psychiatric disorders. They and their colleagues have developed numerous speciality, dual disorder treatment programs at the University of Pittsburgh Medical Center at Western Psychiatric Institute and Clinic (WPIC) in Pittsburgh, Pennsylvania. Dr. Thase also has extensive research experience in the treatment of psychiatric illness and addictions. Both Dr. Thase and Mr. Daley currently are involved in two NIDA-sponsored studies. One study is examining psychosocial treatments for cocaine addiction. The second study is focused on developing a specialized treatment for clients with depression and cocaine addiction. Hence, the authors of this manual have extensive clinical, research, and program development experience.

I would like to use this foreword as an opportunity to summarize the basic principles that can improve the effectiveness of treatment for dual diagnosis patients. Because they are so compatible with the operationalized procedures of Daley and Thase, they will act as an excellent introduction to their work.

Treatment Planning for Dual Diagnosis Patients

Effective treatment plans for dual diagnosis patients integrate the following components: (1) *disorder specific clinical models* for managing the symptoms of chemical dependency and mental and personality disorders; (2) *physical interventions* for managing physical problems related to the target problems; (3) *cognitive therapy* for changing irrational thoughts that drive the target problem; (4) *affective therapy* for changing unmanageable feelings that drive the target problem; (5) *behavioral therapy* for changing self-defeating behaviors that drive the target problem; and (6) *social/situational therapy* for changing lifestyle factors that drive the target problem.

Coexisting Disorders

Dual disorders are best conceptualized as *coexisting disorders* that are interrelated and require simultaneous treatment. It is generally not helpful to try to determine which disorder is primary and which is secondary. It is more productive to profile the patient's physical, psychological, and social symptoms and then develop a treatment plan to stabilize the symptoms of both disorders simultaneously.

As a general rule, patients must stop using alcohol and drugs of abuse before any form of treatment can be effective. Chemical dependency is present in 40-60 percent of all mental health patients. It is therefore recommended that all mental health patients be screened for substance abuse and dependency. Once diagnosed, the first goal is to get the patient abstinent.

Patients with severe mental and personality disorders cannot recover from chemical dependency until they achieve a stable mental status. This requires the stabilization of the severe debilitating symptoms that are interfering with rational thought, emotional management, and behavior self-control. In some cases the stabilization of the mental and personality disorder may require the use of appropriately prescribed psychoactive medication.

As can be seen, the dual disorder patient suffering from both chemical dependency and related mental and personality disorders will need to be simultaneously detoxified and psychiatrically stabilized. These two procedures should be conducted simultaneously.

Effective clinical systems integrate a biopsychosocial model for diagnosis, a developmental model of recovery for treatment planning, and a relapse prevention therapy model for identifying and managing the problems that lead to relapse. We will briefly review each.

The Biopsychosocial Model

The biopsychosocial model for dual disorders isolates physical, psychological, and social symptoms related to the chemical dependency and related mental and personality disorders. The physical symptoms often involve brain chemistry imbalances that can be corrected with the use of psychotropic medication. The psychological symptoms include problems with thinking, emotional management, and behavior. The social symptoms include problems with work, friends, and family.

The Developmental Model of Recovery (DMR)

The Developmental Model of Recovery (DMR) divides recovery into six stages:
- Transition
- Stabilization
- Early Recovery
- Middle Recovery
- Late Recovery
- Maintenance

Relapse Prevention Therapy (RPT)

Relapse is a real possibility for many dual diagnosis patients at any stage of the recovery process. Any stressor or sudden change can elevate stress and trigger the progressive cycle of self-defeating behaviors that lead to relapse. Relapse prevention therapy (RPT) is a specialized method that helps patients to identify and manage relapse warning signs and to intervene early should relapse occur. For most dual recovery patients, there is a process called *reciprocal relapse.* Relapse into chemical addiction will usually trigger a relapse into the mental disorders. Relapse into the symptoms of the mental disorder will usually activate craving for alcohol and other drugs.

Dennis Daley's Dual Diagnosis Workbooks

As you will see, *Dual Diagnosis Recovery Counseling* and the companion guide for clients, *Dual Diagnosis Workbook,* are powerful resources for bringing these concepts to life. The counseling manual and client workbook have been carefully developed and revised based on the clinical experiences of Mr. Daley and Dr. Thase. The methods have been shown to work. I am impressed with these books because they are practical tools that can be used with clients and their families. The clinical principles are sound, and they are presented in a clear, concise, and easy-to-understand way. If used as designed they can form the basis of effective dual diagnosis treatment. I wish you well in exploring the concepts and procedures and putting them to work in helping dual recovery patients and their families to recover.

Terence T. Gorski

Preface

In recent years there has been increasing focus on treating clients who suffer from the dual disorders of psychiatric illness and chemical dependency (addiction). While traditional methods of treatment for psychiatric or addictive disorders have helped numerous clients, many have not experienced the full potential benefits of treatment because the focus was primarily on only one disorder, either the psychiatric illness or the addiction. This approach is not adequate for many dual diagnosis clients who come to treatment with a multiplicity of problems caused or worsened by either or both of their disorders.

This counseling manual was written to provide a framework for mental health and chemical dependency counselors who take care of dual diagnosis clients day in and day out. It is intended to be a "practical" manual that can be adapted to current counseling practices. We recommend that counselors use whatever parts of this manual they believe can help them improve their practice and more adequately meet the complex treatment needs of dual diagnosis clients.

The impetus for this counseling manual came from numerous experiences and sources. First, along with several colleagues from around the country, Dennis D. Daley was invited by the National Institute of Drug Abuse (NIDA) to a one-day meeting in July 1993 during which we each presented a "Counseling Approach" relevant to the problems of addiction. This meeting was moderated by Lisa Onken, Ph.D., and Jack Blaine, M.D., from NIDA, and Kathleen Carroll, Ph.D., from Yale University. The intent of the meeting was to have presenters "concretize" specific treatment approaches in a way that others could easily understand. This current *Dual Disorders Recovery Counseling Manual* is a significant expansion of the version originally presented at this NIDA meeting. In this manual, we follow the "Format for Description of Counseling Approaches" that NIDA provided to each of the presenters as a framework to use. As you will see when you read this manual, it is a very practical and relevant approach that covers many important areas of the counseling process in an easy-to-read format.

Second, for the past several years we have been involved in a National Institute of Drug Abuse multisite clinical trial studying "Psychosocial Treatments of Cocaine Addiction." Three manualized forms of individual treatment are used in this study: Individual Drug Counseling, Supportive-Expressive Psychotherapy, and Cognitive Behavioral Therapy; and a manualized Group Drug Counseling approach is also used. The use of specific, manualized treatments has been found useful by clinicians from a variety of professional disciplines. In addition, Michael E. Thase has been involved in developing cognitive-behavioral treatments for inpatients and outpatients with mood disorders.

Third, throughout the past seven years, we have been involved in developing and implementing dual diagnosis treatment programs in inpatient, partial hospital, and outpatient settings. We were one of the first groups in this country to develop specific treatment programs for dual diagnosis clients in a psychiatric treatment setting. We have changed and fine-tuned our dual diagnosis treatments based on extensive clinical experience with thousands of clients with all types and combinations of psychiatric and chemical dependency disorders. We have also adapted our dual diagnosis treatments based on current realities imposed by managed care, which has led to a significant reduction in the average length of stay in treatment. This program development and clinical work has exposed us to all aspects of treatment for dual disorders throughout the continuum of care.

Fourth, our work in these clinical and research arenas has included significant time providing individual and group supervision to professionals from a variety of disciplines. From this, we have gained a good sense of the knowledge and skill needs of clinicians who work with dual diagnosis clients day in and day out.

Fifth, for several years Dennis Daley regularly met with dual diagnosis clients in our various treatment programs in order to elicit their feedback on what they liked best and least about treatment in our programs. Clients gave their frank opinions on what we were and were not doing so well. This input has been especially instructive and has helped us improve our clinical programming. Over the years, after talking with hundreds and hundreds of clients, certain key themes emerged over and over again, leading to the conclusion that we definitely were on the right track in terms of our clinical programs. We also knew that we had to continue improving services to address the needs of this complex clinical population.

Sixth, we have written a number of workbook and recovery manuals for clients and families, including a comprehensive manual by Dennis Daley entitled *Dual Diagnosis Workbook: Recovery Strategies for Addiction and Mental Health Problems* (Herald House/Independence Press, 1994). This counseling manual describes some ways the client workbook can be used. Most of the workbook sections are described in chapter nine of this DDRC manual. This counseling manual should make it easier for counselors to use this practical client-oriented recovery workbook, especially those conducting group treatment sessions.

Seventh, in our teaching and lecturing within the University of Pittsburgh Medical Center and throughout the United States and Canada, we get a chance to talk to many professionals in mental health, chemical dependency, and dual diagnosis treatment settings. This has allowed us to hear the problems, concerns, and needs of other professionals in the area of dual diagnosis treatment. These experiences have reinforced our belief in the need for a practical and realistic model of treatment that can be adapted to various subgroups of dual diagnosis clients.

In this DDRC model of treatment, we draw on the professional and self-help literature related to psychiatric illness and recovery, addictive illness and recovery, and dual disorders and recovery. We see this process of presenting the DDRC model as simply a beginning. We expect further clinical and research experience to lead to refining and improving this model of treatment over time.

There are several limitations of this counseling manual. First, it does not review specific criteria for various psychiatric or addictive illnesses. We assume the reader is either familiar with these disorders or has access to other books that review specific diagnostic criteria. Second, although this was written to provide a practical overview of a model of counseling, it does not address gender or cultural diversity issues. The reader is encouraged to continuously consider gender and ethnicity issues in counseling practice. And third, while this book provides a framework for conducting DDRC sessions it does not address the clinical nuances and issues specific to the many different types of psychiatric disorders. It is assumed that counselors using this manual will have access to training and/or supervision that will assist them in understanding how to adapt concepts discussed in this manual to different diagnostic groups of clients. Despite these or other limitations, it is our belief that this practical manual will aid counselors in helping clients with dual disorders.

Dennis C. Daley, M.S.W.
Michael E. Thase, M.D.

CHAPTER ONE
Introduction and Overview of the DDRC
Model of Treatment

Introduction

There is significant research evidence that many clients suffer from the dual disorders of psychiatric illness and addiction.[1-3] For recovery to progress, treatment needs to address both disorders. Traditionally, the treatment systems have been dichotomized with clients receiving psychiatric care in the mental health system and addiction treatment in the chemical dependency system. Unfortunately, many clients with dual disorders are never properly diagnosed and/or treated. Mental health systems often fail to address comorbid substance use disorders. Similarly, addiction treatment systems often fail to address comorbid psychiatric disorders. It isn't unusual for clients to get "lost in the shuffle" back and forth between treatment systems.

Because comorbidity is a rather common phenomenon in both mental health and addictive treatment systems, a model of treatment is needed that can address both disorders. This treatment model needs to be flexible and comprehensive so that clients can receive comprehensive and integrated care.

Dual Disorders Recovery Counseling (DDRC) is an integrated approach to treatment of clients who have a substance use disorder and a comorbid psychiatric disorder. The DDRC model of treatment draws on information from the addiction, psychiatric, and dual diagnosis literature such as:

- Individual Drug Counseling and Other Therapies for Addiction[4-6]
- Group Drug Counseling[7]
- Psychiatric Interventions[8-13]
- Relapse Prevention and Skills Training[14-20]
- Family Treatments[4, 21-27]
- Dual Diagnosis Treatments[2, 28-31]
- Self-help Support Groups[32-34]

Psychiatric disorders vary in their severity and effects on the client. While some psychiatric disorders are chronic and persistent with multiple adverse sequelae, other disorders are experienced as a single episode and do not have implications for life-long involvement in recovery. Addictive disorders also vary in terms of severity, chronicity, adverse effects on the client and family, and treatment implications.

While specific types of psychiatric and addictive disorders create specific problems for the client and family, here are many general aspects of dual disorders and recovery. These general aspects are applicable to various combinations of disorders.

The problems and recovery needs of a particular client will depend on the type and severity of the substance use and psychiatric disorders, ego strength and overall psychological functioning, social and family support systems, and internal motivation to change. Although everyone can change in some ways, the more chronically impaired clients have more difficulty in terms of achieving sobriety, maintaining sobriety, coping with psychiatric symptoms, and coping with life problems caused or worsened by their dual disorders.

Goals and Objectives of DDRC

The goals of the DDRC model are:

1. Achievement and maintenance of abstinence from alcohol or other drugs of abuse; or, for clients unable or unwilling to work towards total abstinence, reduction of amount and frequency of use and concomitant biopsychosocial sequelae associated with substance use.
2. Stabilization from acute psychiatric symptoms.
3. Resolution or reduction of psychiatric symptoms and problems.
4. Improvement in functioning: physical, emotional, social, family, interpersonal, occupational, academic, spiritual, financial, and legal.
5. Improved cognitive, behavioral, and interpersonal coping skills.
6. Positive lifestyle change.
7. Early intervention in the process of relapse to either the substance use or psychiatric disorder.

Rationale and Mechanism of Action for DDRC Model

This treatment model is based on the rationale that integrated treatment is the best approach to helping the client with dual disorders. Although the client may use a specific form of treatment at times (e.g., an addiction rehabilitation program to initiate abstinence and set the foundation of recovery), treatment generally focuses on both psychiatric and substance use issues. This dual focus of treatment reduces the chances that an untreated disorder will increase vulnerability to relapse to another disorder.

The DDRC approach involves a broad range of clinical interventions including the following:

- Motivating the client to seek detoxification or inpatient treatment if symptoms warrant; and facilitating an involuntary commitment for psychiatric care if needed.
- Educating the client and family about psychiatric illness, addictive illness, treatment, and the recovery process.
- Supporting the client's efforts at recovery and providing a sense of hope regarding positive change.
- Referring the client for other needed services (case management, medical, social, vocational, economic, housing, etc.).
- Helping the client increase his/her self-awareness so that information regarding dual disorders can be understood in a personal way.
- Helping the client identify problems and areas of change.
- Helping the client develop or improve ability to problem solve, and develop recovery coping skills.

- Facilitating pharmacotherapy evaluation and compliance. This requires close collaboration with the team psychiatrist.
- Engaging the family in the treatment process when appropriate.

Agents of Change

The DDRC model assumes that change may occur as a result of the client/counselor relationship and the team relationship (i.e., team of counselor, psychiatrist, psychologist, nurse and/or other professionals such as case manager, family therapist, etc.). A positive therapeutic alliance is seen as very critical in helping the client get and stay involved in the recovery process. Community support systems, professional treatment groups, and self-help programs also serve as possible agents of positive change for dual diagnosed clients. For the more chronically and persistently mentally ill clients, a case manager functions as an important agent in the change process.

Although the client has to work on a variety of intrapersonal and interpersonal issues as part of long-term recovery, medications facilitate this process by attenuating acute symptoms, improving mood, cognitive abilities, or impulse control. Thus medications may eliminate or reduce symptoms as well as help the client become more able to address problems during counseling sessions (e.g., a severely depressed client may be unable to focus on learning cognitive or behavioral interventions until he/she experiences a certain degree of remission from depressed symptoms; a floridly psychotic client will not be able to focus on abstinence from drugs until the psychotic symptoms are under control).

Etiology and Causative Factors

Both psychiatric and addictive illnesses are viewed as biopsychosocial disorders. These disorders or diseases are caused and/or maintained by a variety of biological, psychological, and cultural/social factors. The degree of influence of specific factors may vary among individuals with dual disorders.

Biological factors include genetic influences, differences in the structure of the brain or in the neurotransmitters in the brain. Many psychiatric disorders such as bipolar illness and schizophrenia and substance use disorders such as alcoholism run in families. These disorders are often more prevalent among offspring who have a parent or sibling with one of these disorders. There is evidence that the brain structure or the ways the neurotransmitters work differs in individuals with certain types of disorders compared to others who do not have these disorders.

Psychological factors also contribute to psychiatric or substance use disorders. These include belief systems, personality traits, and ability to cope with life problems and stresses. Some individuals are more vulnerable to ordinary life stresses than others. Others are much more resilient and able to bounce back from life problems and stresses.

Cultural/social factors can contribute to psychiatric or substance use disorders. These include personal experiences and environmental influences such as family and community . For example, a significant loss of relationship can contribute to depression or the need to escape emotional pain through the use of alcohol or drugs.

Relationships between Psychiatric Illness and Substance Use

This DDRC model assumes that there are several possible relationships between psychiatric illness and substance use.[35-37] These include:

- Axis I and II psychopathology may serve as a *risk factor* for addictive disorders. For example, the odds of having an addictive disorder among individuals with a mental illness is 2.7 according to the National Institute of Mental Health's Epidemiologic Catchment Area (ECA) survey. This means that, compared to a person with no mental disorder, an individual with a mental health disorder is almost three times more likely to have a substance use disorder.

- Addiction is a *risk factor* for psychiatric illness. For example, the odds of having a psychiatric disorder among those with a drug use disorder is 4.5 according to the ECA survey. This means that drug abusers are four and one-half times more likely to have a psychiatric diagnosis compared to non drug abusers.

- Clients with psychiatric disorders are more vulnerable than others to the adverse effects of alcohol or other drugs.

- The use of drugs can precipitate an underlying psychiatric condition. For example, PCP or cocaine use may trigger a first manic episode in a vulnerable individual.

- Psychopathology may *modify the course* of an addictive disorder in terms of:

   a. Rapidity of course: earlier age depressives experience addiction problems earlier; and male-limited alcoholics with antisocial behaviors have earlier onset of addiction compared to milieu-limited alcoholics.[38]

   b. Response to treatment: clients with antisocial or borderline personality disorder often drop out of treatment early.

   c. Symptom picture and long-term outcome: "high psychiatric severity" clients, as measured by the Addiction Severity Index, do worse than "low psychiatric severity" clients;[39] there is a *strong* association between relapse and psychiatric impairment among opiate addicts, and *some* association between relapse and psychiatric impairment among alcoholics.[40]

- Psychiatric symptoms can develop in the course of chronic intoxications. For example, psychosis may follow PCP use or chronic stimulant use or, suicidality and depression may follow a cocaine crash.

- Psychiatric symptoms can emerge as a *consequence of chronic use* of substances or a relapse. For example, depression may be caused by an awareness of the losses associated with addiction, or depression may follow a drug/alcohol relapse.

- Substance-using behavior and psychopathological symptoms, regardless of which came first, *will become meaningfully linked* over the course of time.

- The addictive disorder and psychiatric disorder can develop at different points in time and not be linked. For example, a bipolar client may become hooked on drugs years after being stable from a manic disorder, or an alcoholic may develop panic disorder or major depression long after being sober.

- Symptoms of one disorder can contribute to relapse of the other disorder. For example, an increase in anxiety or hallucinations may lead a client with schizophrenia to alcohol or other drug use to ameliorate symptoms; a cocaine or alcohol binge may lead to depressive symptoms or suicidality.

CHAPTER TWO
Developmental Model of Recovery

Stages of the Change Process

Researchers and clinicians have outlined stages of the change process for psychological problems,[41] addictive disorders,[19, 41-44] and dual disorders.[29, 30] Although each specific model of the change process is somewhat different, each views change as occurring in stages or phases. Each phase of change typically involves several recovery tasks for the client and interventions for professionals providing therapy.

The DDRC model is based on the assumption that there are six possible phases of treatment that clients may progress through over time. These developmental phases are rough guidelines that delineate some typical issues that clients deal with pertinent to the psychiatric illness and the addiction at various points in recovery. Because of the variability of severity and chronicity of dual disorders, motivation to change, internal resources, and external support, not all clients will progress through these phases in the same manner or in a linear fashion. Some clients will move back and forth between phases as their conditions worsen or improve. Others will never move much beyond the first several phases. Nevertheless, these phases provide a clinical and recovery framework from which to approach dual disorders treatment.

Following is a listing of these phases and the approximate time a client may be in each phase. The time frame is very rough because there is much variation among individuals. This is followed by a discussion of recovery issues associated with each phase of dual recovery. Case examples are provided at the end of each phase, illustrating how some clients successfully negotiate a particular phase and how others struggle and have difficulty moving through a specific phase. As managed care continues to influence the duration of treatment, the time available to treat clients is likely to shorten. This will require clinicians to limit the number of sessions provided, which in turn will influence the focus of therapeutic interventions.

Phase 1 - Transition and Engagement (up to several weeks or longer)
Phase 2 - Stabilization (up to several weeks or longer)
Phase 3 - Early Recovery (up to three to six months after stabilization)
Phase 4 - Middle Recovery (six + months following early recovery)
Phase 5 - Late Recovery (year+ after middle recovery)
Phase 6 - Maintenance (ongoing)

Phase 1: Transition and Engagement

This phase of recovery involves becoming engaged in treatment, either voluntarily or as a result of an involuntary commitment. This involves some recognition by the client of an inability to control the use of alcohol or other drugs. It also involves recognition that the psychiatric disorder requires treatment. However, in cases of involuntary commitment involving severe psychiatric decompensation, recognition may not occur until there is some stability of the crisis leading to engagement in treatment and stabilization of acute psychiatric symptoms.

13

Alcohol or drug use can play a major role in triggering a new episode of psychiatric illness following a period of remission that eventuates in a client reentering treatment. Or substance use may lead to a worsening of existing psychiatric symptoms such as depression, mania, psychosis, suicidality, anxiety, panic, out-of-control or threatening behaviors toward others, or an inability to function and take care of basic needs. In some cases alcohol or drug use may "mask" psychiatric symptoms, prolonging the client's entry into treatment.

During this transition and engagement phase, the client begins to recognize that an untreated psychiatric disorder interferes with his or her ability to remain sober from alcohol or other drugs, or it negatively affects motivation and desire to recover from addiction. This phase involves engaging in professional treatment in a psychiatric hospital or outpatient setting, or an addiction rehabilitation setting, depending on the nature and severity of the symptoms of the dual disorders. If the client enters treatment through a psychiatric system, he or she may eventually be referred to an addiction rehabilitation program if it is thought that this is essential in building a foundation of recovery from addiction.

In this phase the client begins to come to grips with mixed feelings about recovery, accepting the reality that the *healthy part* wants to stop using chemicals and get well, and the *sick and addicted part* doesn't want to stop using chemicals or make any changes. The same holds true for the psychiatric illness—the client begins to accept that part of him/her needs help and part doesn't think any help is needed.

If possible the family should get involved in assessment and treatment early in the process. This is best accomplished by assuming the stance that family involvement is important and expected, then conveying to the client that the treatment team would like to invite the family in for sessions. The client can be told that the more the family understands about dual disorders and recovery, the more supportive they can be for the client. The counselor can also stress that family members who attend sessions often find it helpful in addressing some of their questions, concerns, and feelings. Family members or significant others can provide helpful information to professionals who care for the client, provide emotional support to the client, and can gain much from treatment for themselves. The earlier they get involved in the assessment and treatment processes, the better it usually is for everyone involved. Engagement of the family requires patience and aggressiveness on the part of the counselor. Outreach efforts are often needed to get the family to attend assessment or treatment sessions. When families attend individual family sessions with one or more members of the treatment team, they can be asked specific questions about the client's functioning within the family. In addition, the family can be encouraged to share their questions, concerns, and feelings regarding what it was like for them. Families can be invited to multiple family groups or family psychoeducational workshops to gain additional information about specific types of disorders, the recovery process, treatment approaches, and the family's role in treatment. These services often give the family members a chance to be heard and gain support from others.

During this phase of treatment, the client begins to accept the need for a recovery program that involves a combination of professional treatment and self-help programs such as AA, NA, CA, DRA, or other mental health support groups. The client learns that help and support from others is needed in order to recover from the dual disorders. The client's motivation to change initially may be external during this recovery phase as he/she gets involved in recovery mainly because of the problems the addiction and mental health disorder have caused. Or, the client engages in treatment because he/she was *forced* or *pressured* to accept help by the family, an employer, the court system, a health care or social service professional, or some other important person such as a close friend.

This transition and engagement phase may take up to several weeks, although for some it takes longer to become truly engaged in dual diagnosis recovery and motivated to change. Some clients enter treatment only to drop out early. If clients make a commitment to stay in recovery, even if they feel their motivation is questionable, they put themselves in a good position to benefit from treatment. Keep in mind that many people need time to develop their motivation to recover, and that staying in treatment "buys time" for the client to develop this motivation and see the many potential benefits of treatment.

Case #1: Michael is a 34-year-old married, employed father of two children who was involuntarily committed to a psychiatric hospital following a manic episode. During his manic episode Michael's judgment became severely impaired. He became irrational and threatened to kick his wife and children out of their home, insisted he was going to take over a business in another state and quit going to work, started drinking after two years of sobriety, and eventually got arrested for trying to solicit teenagers to have sex with him. The police initiated an involuntary commitment when it was clear that Michael was out of touch with reality and a threat to others. Once his mood and behavior stabilized during his hospitalization, Michael realized the seriousness of his condition and impact on his behavior and agreed to continue outpatient treatment for his bipolar illness. He recognized that his psychiatric illness also contributed to an alcohol relapse and agreed he needed to abstain from alcohol. During inpatient treatment, his family attended several family psychoeducational groups to gain information about dual disorders, the impact on families, and recovery strategies. He also had sessions with his family and members of his treatment team to discuss the impact of his behaviors on his wife and kids, their feelings and reactions, and ongoing recovery strategies. His wife was encouraged to resume Al-Anon participation as this had been helpful to her in the past.

Case #2: Charles is a 41-year-old, divorced father of three with a long history of multiple psychiatric hospitalizations, rehabilitation programs, and outpatient treatment. He has been treated for recurrent depression, antisocial personality disorder, heroin addiction, alcoholism, and more recently, crack/cocaine addiction. Although Charles has had periods of sobriety for more than a year, and periods of stable psychiatric functioning in the past since getting addicted to crack two years ago, he has been unable to stay drug free for more than a month. During the past two years, he has been hospitalized three times for depression and suicide attempts. Unfortunately, Charles always drops out of outpatient or partial hospital programs before becoming engaged in treatment. His pattern is to attend a few outpatient or partial hospital sessions with many cancellations and no-shows. He usually returns briefly to treatment when he "needs" something or is in a crisis resulting from his drug use or depressive symptomatology. Even multiple efforts at outreach have had a limited impact on Charles's ability to engage in treatment.

Phase 2: Stabilization from Acute Symptoms of Dual Disorders

This phase involves stabilizing from the acute psychiatric symptoms. In this phase, the client probably will receive medications to help stabilize acute and severe psychiatric symptoms. Depending on the nature of the symptoms and past response to medications, it may take several weeks or even longer for medications to work effectively in reducing or eliminating acute psychiatric symptoms. This requires patience on the part of the client and a willingness to stick with treatment even if he/she feels frustrated because symptoms are not remitting quickly enough. In some cases stabilizing from an episode of psychiatric illness is a relatively smooth process. In other cases it is much more complex and takes longer. The counselor also needs to be patient and provide support and education to help the client through this process.

The stabilization phase involves getting alcohol and drugs out of the client's system and adjusting to being chemically free. For some people, detoxification in an inpatient or outpatient setting is needed in order to break the cycle of addictive chemical use.

Acute symptoms of withdrawal from alcohol or other drugs usually last only a few days to a week. The specific withdrawal symptoms experienced depend on the amount and types of chemicals the client has been using as well as how long chemicals have been used.

Protracted, or post-acute withdrawal symptoms, on the other hand, may last for weeks or months. If the client's body was used to heavy use of alcohol or other drugs for years and years, he/she cannot expect to adjust to being chemically free in just a few short days.

Acquiring information about the addictive and psychiatric illnesses, the role of professional therapy, the role of medications, and the role of self-help programs in ongoing recovery is an essential component of this stabilization phase. The client learns about his/her specific diagnoses, causes of psychiatric and addictive illnesses, effects of dual disorders, and steps to take to cope with the dual disorders. The more information the client learns, the more empowered he/she will feel and the more aware he/she will become of the course of recovery as it relates to the specific illnesses that he/she has, as well as what steps can be taken to help oneself. The client plays a very important role in the treatment team and needs to make a sincere effort to get well if recovery is to progress.

In this phase of recovery, the client begins to learn ways to cope with addictive thinking, cravings to use alcohol or drugs, and symptoms of the psychiatric illness. In addition to involvement in professional treatment, the client gets involved in self-help programs such as AA, NA, CA, Women For Sobriety (WFS), Rational Recovery (RR) for the addiction, Double Trouble, MISA, SAMI, CAMI, or Dual Recovery Anonymous (DRA) programs for dual disorders; Emotions Anonymous (EA), Recovery, Inc., for any type of emotional problem; or mental support groups based on a specific psychiatric illness (e.g., anxiety disorder support groups, manic-depression support groups, etc.). Decisions about specific types of support groups to attend should be a mutual decision between the client, counselor, and treatment team.

As the client progresses through this phase of recovery, he/she becomes less preoccupied with alcohol and other drugs. The client learns ways to counteract euphoric recall and other positive thoughts about using chemicals, which reduces the risk of relapsing to chemical use. Very importantly, the client begins to see that recovery is possible, and despite whatever psychiatric illness he/she has, there are effective treatments that can reduce or eliminate symptoms and help improve functioning.

16

The client's motivation gets stronger in this phase as he/she learns that there are many steps that can be taken to help recovery progress. There is a greater degree of comfort in accepting help and support from others such as professionals, sponsors and members of support programs, and family members.

A major aspect of this phase is accepting the need for long-term involvement in professional treatment and self-help recovery. The client works closely with the counselor and treatment team in developing a list of problems to work on, prioritizing these problems, and developing problem-solving strategies to begin addressing select problems from this list. The client accepts the need for total abstinence from alcohol, street drugs, and non-prescribed drugs as the path to take in recovery. There is a recognition that use of any alcohol or drugs can interfere with psychiatric recovery, lead the client back to the primary drug of abuse, or cause another addiction to develop.

The client's family should continue involvement in this phase as well. The degree they are involved and the nature of their involvement depends on the client's disorders and treatment needs, the family's treatment needs, and the recommendations of the counselor and other professionals providing treatment. Excluding the family from ongoing involvement in recovery can lead to serious problems later.

This phase of recovery may take anywhere from a few weeks to several months. The ease in which the client moves through this stage depends on the severity of the psychiatric illness and addiction. Again, the importance of addressing both the addiction and psychiatric illness must be stressed because it will be extremely hard to stabilize and get well if both disorders aren't addressed in recovery.

Case #1: Faye is a 59-year-old divorced, unemployed mother of two daughters and one son. She sought treatment for chronic depression, chronic anxiety, family problems, and alcoholism. During the first four months of treatment, she cancelled most of her outpatient sessions and continued to drink alcohol on a daily basis despite experiencing severe symptoms of depression and anxiety. When she finally accepted the fact that her alcohol use was a major factor in her inability to improve her anxiety and depression, she reluctantly agreed to enter the hospital for detoxification and medication evaluation. Once she was stabilized, Faye became involved regularly in outpatient treatment and was able to focus both on staying sober and reducing her anxiety and depression.

Case #2: Twanda is a 28-year-old single woman with a history of schizophrenia, alcoholism, and polysubstance abuse (pot, cocaine, and many pills). During periods of active chemical use, Twanda decompensates and becomes psychotic. Before this, she uses chemicals, stops taking psychiatric medications, stops attending partial hospital programming, and seldom keeps her appointments with her treatment team. Her condition recently worsened following six months of fairly stable functioning when she started drinking on a daily basis. Twanda refused to stop drinking and occasionally showed up at the clinic, often smelling of alcohol. She stopped taking her medications and refused to enter the hospital. Twanda did not stabilize until an involuntary commitment was initiated after she stopped eating and threatened to kill herself.

Phase 3: Early Recovery

This phase of recovery involves continued work at recovery from both of the disorders. The client works at staying sober by learning practical ways of coping with cravings and desires to use chemicals. And, he/she learns to avoid people, places, and things that represent a relapse risk for addiction. Because the client cannot avoid all risk factors, he/she slowly begins to learn nonchemical ways of coping with pressures from others to use alcohol or other drugs, and how to cope with situations that in the past led to using chemicals. The client becomes more used to sobriety and coping with the many physical, emotional, and social adjustments that it brings.

During this phase, the client begins to make *internal changes* by learning how to challenge and change addictive thinking. He/she also begins incorporating new sobriety based values that help to strengthen the commitment to treatment. The *sober* side takes a stronger role than the *addicted* side and the client more openly embraces the need for a recovery program that accepts total abstinence as the best goal. He/she may still want to use alcohol or other drugs at times but understands and accepts this as a normal aspect of addictive disease. The client knows that he/she can cope with this addicted self by using the *tools of the program* learned to this point.

During early recovery clients begin to learn new ways of coping with the psychiatric disorder and the problems it caused in life. They learn that while medication can help improve some of the symptoms of the psychiatric illness, they still have to work hard at making changes in themselves and their lifestyle in order to achieve a better and more fulfilling recovery.

The client learns to challenge and change negative thinking that previously contributed to anxiety, depression, or unhappiness. He/she becomes more realistic about recovery and the need for active involvement in a program of change. During this phase the client also learns to change some behaviors, especially ones that caused difficulties in the past. There is an increased awareness of the role of behaviors, thinking, and personality in the development and maintenance of the psychiatric disorder.

Early recovery also involves building structure and regularity into day-to-day life so that the client keeps busy, stays focused on recovery issues, gets involved in leisure activities that are enjoyable, and doesn't have a lot of free time. Structure helps the client stay focused on goals and can serve as a protective factor against relapse to the psychiatric illness or the addiction.

In family sessions the focus is on understanding the impact of the dual disorders and behaviors on the family. Initially this is difficult and exacerbates feelings of guilt and shame. Family sessions aid the family in learning how they can support the client's recovery and what they should not do. Both the client and family learn to communicate more openly about recovery issues. This work with the family helps set the stage for the client to make amends later in the recovery process.

Involvement in therapy and self-help support programs helps the client deal with these or other pertinent issues during this phase of recovery. Working the 12 Steps becomes an important aspect of the change plan. So does working with a sponsor who guides the client in using the tools of recovery. As the client progresses through this stage, he/she feels less guilty and shameful and comes to see oneself not as a "bad person" but as an "ill person" whose disorders contributed to behaviors that were problematic. The client accepts responsibility for coping with the dual disorders by staying involved in professional treatment and self-help programs. It becomes clear that

18

ongoing help and support from others is still needed because recovery is difficult and presents many challenges.

Early recovery involves roughly the first three to six months after the stabilization phase. As with previous phases, some clients work through this phase more easily than others. If the client relapses to alohol or drug use, or experiences a worsening of psychiatric symptoms during this phase, he/she will need to restabilize before the issues discussed above can be adequately addressed in treatment sessions.

Case #1: Janet is a 40-year-old married mother of two daughters. This is her second involvement in outpatient treatment for severe anxiety and panic symptoms, post-traumatic stress disorder, and drug addiction (tranquilizers and pot). During her first outpatient treatment, she never addressed her addiction and received limited benefit from medications and psychotherapy. Janet currently has been sober for two months. She attends individual and group sessions weekly and is seen with her family every several weeks. She takes medication for her anxiety and panic symptoms, and is learning to cope with exacerbations of symptoms without constantly seeking medications. Janet is realizing that while medications can help, they cannot alleviate all of her symptoms or problems; and there is no "magic bullet" for all that ails her. She also attends AA meetings and has found it helpful to spend time at a local recovery club. She's been able to cope with several "close calls" and social pressures to use drugs. When Janet feels close to using, she reminds herself that her daughters suffer when she gets high because she becomes irresponsible and spends most of her time away from home. In individual treatment sessions Janet is focusing on her pattern of negative thinking and ways to challenge anxious, depressed, and angry thoughts. In family sessions Janet is focusing on improving communication and controlling anger toward her mother.

Case #2: Stan is a 20-year-old college student diagnosed with schizotypal personality disorder, depression, alcohol dependence, and polysubstance abuse (primarily marijuana and PCP). He was hospitalized briefly following a psychotic episode. He has not used any substances since being discharged from the hospital five months ago and is active in AA and outpatient therapy. He has shown moderate improvements in his depressive symptoms and is about 70 percent compliant in taking his antidepressant medications. Stan evidences considerable difficulties in setting goals for himself, structuring his time, and relating to other people. His main emphasis in treatment thus far has been learning to socialize with others without using pot in order to fit in, adding structure to his days so that he doesn't spend most of his time watching TV alone, and coping with persistent feelings of depression. He now attends NA or AA on a daily basis and finally got a sponsor in NA. Stan's mood has improved modestly. He still complains of low motivation and poor interpersonal relationships but is beginning to explore ways to deal with these issues.

Phase 4: Middle Recovery

This phase involves building on the work from the previous early recovery phase. In therapy or counseling sessions the client shares more about his/her inner thoughts and feelings and reaches a greater level of self-awareness. Therapeutic work is directed toward improving interpersonal relationships. This requires learning to communicate more openly with others and nurturing relationships with family, friends, or other significant people in the client's life. As a result of interpersonal change and growth, the client becomes more caring and loving toward others. He/she not only *gets* support and help from others, but also *gives* to others, too. This helps the client develop and maintain balanced relationships that are not one-sided or self-serving.

In middle recovery the client spends more time and effort repairing the damage to relationships and self-esteem caused by the dual disorders and behaviors. Steps 8 and 9 of AA, NA, CA, or DRA are addressed with a sponsor and/or counselor. These steps help the client to identify others hurt by his/her behaviors, become willing to make amends, and figure out ways to make amends in cases where doing so will not bring harm to other people. Relationships become more meaningful and satisfying as a result of this process. In relationships where damage cannot be repaired and the relationships cannot be salvaged, clients have to learn to accept this reality rather than judge themselves harshly.

Spirituality issues in recovery become more important during this phase. The client further develops his/her own unique sense of spirituality and uses this to help recovery and growth. This process may or may not also involve active participation in some formal type of religious practices. Many clients find strength and hope in attending religious services and praying.

As the client progresses through this phase of recovery, the focus gradually shifts more toward becoming a better person and more satisfied with oneself. Steps 10 and 11 in particular help in this process.

The client continues improving coping strategies to deal with negative or upsetting thoughts and feelings during this middle recovery phase. He/she learns to challenge and change anxious, depressed, or other negative thinking patterns, realizing that by changing thoughts and beliefs, feelings and behaviors can be changed, too. Coping strategies strengthen as the client practices new ways of thinking, feeling, and behaving. As positive changes are made, the client's self-esteem rises. He/she feels less demoralized and victimized by the dual disorders. Instead the client sees the need to continue responsibly making changes as part of ongoing recovery. This enables him/her to stop blaming society, bad breaks, bad genes, or others for problems.

Because addictive and psychiatric disorders are often chronic, relapsing illnesses, the client learns to identify and manage warning signs of relapse during this recovery phase. He/she learns that going back to using alcohol and drugs doesn't usually "come out of the blue" but represents a movement away from recovery towards relapse over a period of time. Similarly, the client learns that new episodes of psychiatric illness or significant worsening of persistent and chronic psychiatric symptoms often occur gradually over time. Knowing potential relapse warning signs allows the client to develop recovery strategies that reduce the likelihood of relapse to either or both of the dual disorders. A relapse prevention plan becomes an important part of recovery. By monitoring recovery on a daily basis, the client is in a position to spot relapse warning signs early. This, in turn, allows him/her to take action before things get out of hand.

If the psychiatric illness was a first episode and the client is fairly free of symptoms as a result of treatment, he/she may be withdrawn from medications. Usually, this is not done until the client has been doing well for four months or longer. If the client has a recurrent psychiatric disorder or a chronic, persistent form of illness such as schizophrenia or bipolar disease, he/she most likely will remain on medications, even if doing well. The purpose of medications in such a case is to *prevent* the possibility of a recurrence of psychiatric illness. The idea is similar to taking medications for high blood pressure or other medical illnesses — taking medicine maintains treatment gains and helps prevent future symptoms. It still is possible for symptoms to break through even if the client continues to take medications. However, this happens less often than in cases in which medications are stopped prematurely.

Middle recovery usually involves the six-to-twelve-month period following early recovery. Again, as in other phases, some move through this phase more easily than others.

Case #1: Art is a single, 29-year-old college graduate with an obsessive-compulsive disorder (OCD) and alcoholism. His OCD became so severe that he became paralyzed at work and was unable to complete simple tasks. He eventually lost his job as a result. He finally sought psychiatric treatment at the recommendation of a friend. Art currently takes Anafranil, attends a partial hospital program two days a week, and attends AA three times per week. His OCD symptoms have improved markedly, and Art has been sober for ten months. In treatment he is focusing on becoming comfortable communicating with other people and exploring ways to improve his relationships. He has learned to decrease his high expectations of others, be less critical of himself and others, and is now more positive in his conversations. Art, who initially was quiet and unable to share much support from others, is also working on sharing more support to others and self-disclosing his feelings and struggles. Members of his treatment group, who initially found him to be aloof and intellectual, now find that he fits in more easily and can relate more on a mutual basis than before.

Case #2: Lois is a 52-year-old widowed mother of four in treatment for alcoholism and recurrent depression. She has had periods of sobriety up to three years previously and currently has been sober almost one year. Lois has also had multiple episodes of depression in the past, several of which were precipitated by stopping medications or drinking alcohol. She currently takes antidepressant medications, attends outpatient sessions twice a month, and attends AA three to five times a week. In treatment, Lois is focusing primarily on her patterns of alcohol relapse and recurrences of depression so that she is more aware of early warning signs. Although comfortable with accepting her alcoholism as a chronic disease, she struggles with seeing the chronicity of her depressive illness. Lois is also focusing on developing her spirituality and feels she ignored this aspect of recovery during previous attempts at recovery. She has gotten a sponsor for the first time, and, despite some difficuties opening up and sharing her difficulties, Lois is learning to use her sponsor to help her through rough times. Her sponsor has also helped her figure out ways to make amends to her adult children. Although this initially evoked considerable guilt, Lois' relationships with three of her children have improved. Lois is more realistic and patient with her youngest daughter who still is very angry at her.

Phase 5: Late Recovery

This phase of recovery involves continued work started in the previous phases. Usually, the client gets into personal recovery issues in greater depth as a solid foundation for recovery has been established. During this phase the client focuses more on changing *character defects* and dealing with other problems caused by his/her personality style. He/she builds on personal strengths and works on changing weaknesses.

Late recovery involves working at finding greater meaning in life and developing more positive values. The spiritual and interpersonal aspects of recovery help the client in this quest for meaning. One of the many beautiful aspects of recovery is that it provides the client a chance to become a better, more fulfilled person. But this only comes with patience, discipline, and hard work.

If the client is still in therapy, focus may shift away from practical daily life issues and more toward greater self-exploration so that the client better understands the self: defenses, personality style, patterns of behavior, values, strengths, and vulnerabilities. The client gains greater clarity on how his/her past influences present behavior. Greater self-understanding helps to pave the way to make personal changes and improve the self.

As the client progresses through this phase, he/she becomes more able and willing to focus on healing from past emotional wounds related to growing up in a family in which a serious addiction or mental health problem existed, or related to other traumatic experiences such as incest or other forms of abuse. The client learns to face pain head on rather than use it as a reason to drink alcohol or use drugs, or as a reason not to make changes. Gradually, the client learns to let go of anger, disappointment, sadness, and hate. And he/she begins to learn to forgive others who caused physical or emotional harm in the past. If the client is unable to forgive, he/she has to learn to live with the pain and anger in ways that aren't self-destructive.

In some instances this healing takes place by working the 12-Step program of AA, NA, CA, or DRA. In other cases it involves deeper exploration in therapy sessions. Therapy helps the client slowly work through emotional pain and put the past in a different perspective so that it doesn't continue to cause so much emotional pain. To aid the healing journey, the client may also participate in other types of self-help support groups such as Adult Children of Alcoholics, Incest Survivors Anonymous, or codependency groups.

Late recovery also provides the client with an opportunity to work at "balancing" the various areas of life: recovery, work, love, relationships, fun, and spirituality. This phase roughly involves a year to two after the middle recovery period.

Case #1: John is a 28-year-old, employed, married man with a history of depression starting during his teenage years. His alcohol and drug use worsened considerably so he entered a rehabilitation program and joined AA. John had been sober more than a year when he sought outpatient help for an episode of depression. He benefited from a trial of medications but is now medication free. He initially attended sessions weekly but now comes once each month. In treatment, once his mood was stabilized, John focused on coming to grips with his negative feelings toward his parents, especially his father. John also addressed what he called his "self-centeredness" after his wife became pregnant and he became aware of feeling deeply jealous and worried about not being the center of her attention. His initial negative feelings about fatherhood made him realize he had to address some of his personality issues which he avoided because of his previous perception that he had no serious flaws to change. John also realized he had to be more responsible economically and began looking at ways to handle money better now that he was going to have a child to support. He grew up in a wealthy family and developed very poor money management habits over the years. John has gradually learned to focus less on himself and more on his pregnant wife.

Case #2: Liz is a 42-year-old, single, unemployed woman with borderline personality disorder, depression with psychotic features, and alcoholism. She has been in and out of mental health and addiction treatment programs since she was a teenager as a result of suicide attempts, severe depression, and several psychotic decompensations. After more than a year of good sobriety, she began focusing on sexual abuse issues from the past in therapy sessions and by joining an incest survivor's support group. Several weeks later she became depressed and suicidal after being flooded by awful memories and feelings of intense rage. However, unlike previous times when attempting to deal with her past, Liz was able to appropriately use her therapist, AA sponsor, and support system and dealt with this crisis without getting drunk or entering the psychiatric hospital. These were significant achievements for her. Liz is also learning to rely less on her therapist and more on her social support system during crises, whereas in the past she expected her therapist to virtually be on-call all the time to help her with her frequent crises. Her ability to tolerate distress and negative effects has improved considerably. She is also much less judgmental toward herself and less prone to exaggerating her character flaws at the expense of ignoring her strengths and achievements.

Phase 6: Maintenance

This final phase is best seen as an *ongoing* phase. It involves continued work on the "self" through ongoing work of a recovery program. The client shifts toward more self-reliance during this phase and relies less on others for help and support. The client still needs and depends on others, but more and more he/she is able to rely on inner resources to cope with thoughts, feelings, and problems in life.

Part of continued growth and development may come from "giving away" what was learned in recovery by sponsoring others and working Step 12. Some clients are able to use their experience, hope, and strength to help others in recovery.

Because the client is well-grounded in recovery by this time, he/she is better able to deal with the problems life brings in day-to-day life. These problems are faced head on. Coping with problems and changes in life are not nearly as overwhelming as they were in the earlier phases of recovery.

Throughout recovery clients learn to cope with setbacks and mistakes made in life and recovery. They use these mistakes to learn something new about themselves or life rather than as a reason to put themselves down. Clients become more accepting of their limitations, weaknesses, and flaws. Goals are modified whenever the client discovers they cannot be reached or that they were too high in the first place.

Many illnesses are lifelong conditions. Therefore during the maintenance phase, if the client has a recurrent or persistent form of psychiatric illness, he/she continues taking medications. By this phase the client probably has decreased the frequency in which counselor or psychiatrist is seen as the client is "living the program" of recovery.

As the name of this phase implies, it is ongoing. The client maintains gains made previously while continuing to grow as a person.

Case #1: Joan is a 36-year-old, married mother of two sons who sought help for alcoholism and agoraphobia with panic attacks after many years of being virtually symptom free and sober. She called five treatment programs before finding one that agreed to treat her. By the time she sought treatment, she had lost her job and had immense trouble leaving her home except for the most essential things such as shopping for groceries. Due to her high level of alcohol use and prior history of severe withdrawal symptoms, Joan was detoxified and stabilized on psychiatric medications. She then participated in regular outpatient sessions and AA meetings and continued taking medications. Following a year of stable recovery, Joan had an alcohol use relapse that lasted two weeks. Fortunately she cut this relapse off quickly and suffered minimal damage in her life. Joan has now been doing very well for more than two years and is seen every three months by her therapist and treatment team for medication checks. She has returned to work, is able to leave home whenever she wants, and seldom experiences any symptoms of her illness. Joan attends AA once or twice a week and feels comfortable coping with infrequent desire to drink alcohol.

Case #2: Patrick is a 27-year-old, married father of two who initially sought help for cocaine addiction and completed a 28-day rehabilitation program. About a year after being drug free, he became depressed and felt vulnerable to using drugs again so he sought outpatient treatment. Because he saw serious problems in his marriage as a factor in his depression, Patrick was seen in both individual and marital sessions. His marriage improved as he and his wife, also in recovery from addiction, learned to face their conflicts head on and accept each other's differences and flaws. Patrick has been clean more than four years and now sponsors three other men in NA. He is using the principles and tools of the 12-Step program in his daily life. After being out of treatment for almost two years, Patrick sought short-term help for recurrent marital conflict. He and his wife were seen for 12 sessions over a six-month period. They were able to use the sessions to improve their relationship. He continues to use his sponsor and the NA program to grow as a person.

PHASE OF TREATMENT	POSSIBLE THERAPEUTIC ISSUES	POSSIBLE THERAPEUTIC INTERVENTIONS	CRITERIA FOR PROGRESS
1. *Transition and Engagement* (weeks or longer)	Establishing diagnoses Resistance of client Ambivalence/denial Acute symptoms of illnesses	Conduct assessment Review effects of disorders Involve family Validate ambivalence Provide motivational counseling Educate about illness and recovery Facilitate referrals Medication evaluation Provide support Introduce 12 Steps	Acknowledges there is a problem with alcohol or drugs Acknowledges there is a mental health problem Agrees to participate in treatment Agrees to participate in self-help programs Stops or reduces substance use
2. *Stabilization* (weeks or longer)	Acute symptoms of illness Denial/minimization/grief Cravings/close calls Need for family and social support	Detoxification/medication Review dual diagnosis history Monitor cravings and psychiatric symptoms Develop problem list Craving management Continue work on 12 Steps Family sessions as needed	Accept dual disorders; increased motivation Feels hopeful about recovery System is alcohol and drug free and withdrawal is over; or there are no more acute withdrawal symptoms Decrease in cravings and preoccupation with using Psychiatric symptoms do not seriously impair ability to function
3. *Early Recovery* (three to six months after Stabilization)	People, places, and things Negative feelings Guilt and shame Persistent psychiatric symptoms Impact on family Negative thinking Need for structure Lapse, relapse, and recurrences	Identify triggers and coping strategies Discuss negative feelings and coping strategies (anger, guilt, etc.) Identify and challenge cognitive distortions and other forms of negative thinking ("stinking" thinking) Leisure counseling Relapse prevention counseling Family sessions as needed Continue work on 12 Steps	Feels less guilty and shameful Increased understanding of disorders (causes, effects, recovery issues, treatment strategies) Improved ability to cope with people, places, and things Improved ability to manage feelings and psychiatric symptoms Continues active involvement in treatment and self-help Connects with a support system and/or sponsor Deals with setbacks; accepts steps toward progress

PHASE OF TREATMENT	POSSIBLE THERAPEUTIC ISSUES	POSSIBLE THERAPEUTIC INTERVENTIONS	CRITERIA FOR PROGRESS
4. **Middle Recovery** (six to twelve months after Early Recovery)	Interpersonal relationships Making amends Upsetting feelings Negative thinking Lapse, relapse, and recurrence Spirituality	Discuss ways to improve relationships and communications Make amends Continue practicing new ways of thinking Relapse education on warning signs and high-risk factors Relapse analysis Daily inventory Discuss spirituality issues May stop medications (for single episode of psychiatric illness) Family session as needed Continue work on 12 Steps	Feels better about self in relationships Improve relationships and communication Thinking is more positive and less critical or hopeless Able to spot early warning signs of relapse Able to recover from lapse, relapse, or recurrence Increased comfort with spiritual aspect of recovery Less reliance on therapist or sponsor
5. **Late Recovery** (1+ years after Middle Recovery)	Continue work from previous phase Healing from emotional wounds of past Confront vs. avoid pain and conflict Forgiveness of others Sponsorship Lifestyle balance (work, play, love, recovery, spirituality, etc.) Personality (character defects)	Discuss ways to enhance meaning in life Reevaluate past experiences to reduce hurt and pain, and forgive others Discuss strategies to identify and face current emotional pain Focus on ways to balance major areas of life Discuss personality traits and strategies to change defects Continue step work	Increase in self-exploration in treatment or with sponsor Increase in self-esteem and confidence Increase in feelings of serenity and satisfaction with life Increase in concern toward others "Gives back" to others through sponsorship and service Less reliant on others and more reliant on self Comfortable with personal strengths and weaknesses Uses the "tools" and "principles" of recovery in daily life
6. **Maintenance**	Continue work from previous phase Focuses on new problems and issues	Focus on continued growth Self-improvement	More balanced and satisfying life Tries to improve self (character, values, goals, coping strategies) and interpersonal relationships Lives the program in daily life

As the case examples on page 25 show, people in recovery vary in their recovery process and the issues that they address during different phases of recovery. These cases show that recovery is not a smooth process in which one moves easily from one phase to another. Rather, issues overlap between phases and clients often experience crises, problems, and setbacks, often going back and forth between phases of recovery. Additionally some clients will not be interested in certain issues such as changing character defects or developing spirituality. Others will not want to use 12-Step programs, sponsors, or other types of support groups. Clinicians must be realistic about the degree of influence that can be exerted on particular clients. While the *ideal* is for clients to broadly address physical, psychological, interpersonal, family, and spiritual issues, the *reality* is that clinicians can work with the client where he/she is and must be careful about "pushing" recovery too hard. Many clients make positive changes even if they do not address all of the issues that clinicians feel are important.

The chart on pages 26–27 summarizes various phases of treatment, possible therapeutic issues, possible therapeutic interventions, and criteria for client progress.

CHAPTER THREE
Format of DDRC

Modalities of Treatment

The DDRC model can be used in a variety of group treatments and in individual treatment. Aspects of this model can be adapted to family treatment as well.

Treatment Settings

This DDRC model was primarily developed for use in a mental health or dual disorders treatment setting. It can be used throughout the continuum of care in inpatient, other residential, partial hospital, and outpatient settings. The specific areas of focus in treatment will depend on the client's presenting problems and symptoms, and the treatment setting. This model can be adapted and used in addiction treatment settings provided that appropriate training, supervision, and consultation are available for the counselor in relation to psychiatric issues.

Duration of Treatment

Acute inpatient dual diagnosis treatment usually lasts up to three weeks. Longer-term speciality residential treatment programs may last from several months to a year or more. Partial hospitalization programs usually last from six to twelve months. Outpatient treatment lasts six months or longer. Recurrent conditions such as certain depressive disorders and bipolar illness, as well as persistent mental illness such as schizophrenia, typically require ongoing participation in maintenance pharmacotherapy and supportive counseling.

With the recent changes brought about as a result of managed care, the trend in treatment is moving away from inpatient care except in the most serious cases of acute illness. Additionally, all treatments are getting shorter in length, requiring clinicians to limit specific issues and problems addressed in counseling sessions. The DDRC model provides a framework and structure that can help clinicians adjust to the changing demands of managed care.

Compatibility with Other Treatments

The DDRC is very compatible with pharmacotherapy and family treatment. Many clients require medication to treat psychiatric symptoms. Therefore, medication compliance, the perception of taking medications as a "recovering alcoholic or addict," and potential adverse effects of alcohol or other drugs on medication efficacy are important issues to discuss with the client.

Family participation in assessment and treatment is viewed as important and compatible with the DDRC model. The family can:

- help provide important information in the assessment process;

- provide support to the recovering client;

- address their questions, concerns, and reactions to coping with the dual diagnosed client;

29

- address their own problems and issues in treatment sessions and/or self-help programs; and

- help identify early signs of addiction relapse or psychiatric recurrence and point these out to the recovering dual diagnosed family member.

A combination of family psychoeducational programs, family counseling sessions, and family support programs can be used to help families. Referrals for assessment of serious problems (psychiatric, substance abuse, behavioral) among specific family members can also be initiated as necessary (e.g., a child of a client who is suicidal, very depressed, or getting in trouble at school can be referred for a psychiatric evaluation and treatment).

Role of Self-Help Programs

Self-help programs are very important in the DDRC model of treatment. All clients are educated regarding self-help programs and linked up to specific programs when appropriate. The self-help programs recommended may include any of the following for a given client: AA, NA, CA,and other addiction support groups such as Rational Recovery or Women for Sobriety; dual recovery support groups; and mental health support groups. However, this model does not assume that a client cannot recover without involvement in a 12-Step group or that failure to attend 12-Step groups is a sign of resistance. The DDRC model assumes that clients may utilize "tools of recovery" of self-help programs even if meetings are not attended. Sponsorship, recovery literature, slogans, and recovery clubs are also seen as very helpful aspects of recovery for dual diagnosed clients.

Clients Best Suited for this Counseling Approach:

The DDRC approach can be adapted for virtually any type of substance use, mental health, or combination of disorders. However, it is best suited for mood, anxiety, schizophrenic, personality, adjustment, and other addictive disorders in combination with a drug and/or alcohol dependence.

Clients Poorly Suited for this Counseling Approach:

Clients with mental retardation, organic brain syndromes, head injuries, and more severe forms of thought disorders are less suited for this counseling approach. However, many individuals with schizophrenic disorders can benefit from various aspects of DDRC.

CHAPTER FOUR
Counselor Characteristics and Training

Educational Requirements

The educational requirements are variable for inpatient staff and depend on one's professional discipline's requirements. Formal education of inpatient staff include M.D., Ph.D., master, bachelor, and associate degrees. Training in fields such as nursing may vary as well and include M.S.N., B.S.N., R.N., and L.P.N. Outpatient therapists tend to have at least a master's degree or higher and function fairly autonomously.

Training, Credentials, and Experience

To effectively provide counseling services to dual diagnosed clients the counselor needs to have a broad knowledge of assessment and treatment of dual disorders. Specific areas with which the counselor should be familiar include the following:

- Psychiatric illnesses (types, causes, symptoms, and effects)
- Substance use disorders (trends in substance abuse, types and effects of various substances, causes, symptoms, and effects of addiction)
- The relationship between the psychiatric illness and substance use
- The recovery process for dual disorders
- Self-help programs (for addiction, mental health disorders, and dual disorders)
- Family issues in treatment and recovery
- Relapse (precipitants, warning signs, and relapse prevention strategies for both disorders)
- Specialized psychosocial treatment approaches for various psychiatric disorders (e.g., treatments for PTSD, obsessive-compulsive disorder, etc.)
- Pharmacotherapy
- The continuum of care (for both addiction and psychiatric illnesses)
- Local community resources
- The process of involuntary hospitalization.
- Motivational counseling strategies
- How to deal with ambivalent clients and those who do not want help
- Strategies to deal with refractory or treatment resistant clients with chronic forms of mental illness
- How to use bibliotherapeutic assignments to facilitate the client's recovery

The counselor must be able to develop a therapeutic alliance with a broad range of clients who manifest different disorders and differing abilities to utilize professional treatment. This requires self-awareness of one's owns issues, biases, limitations, and strengths, as well as a willingness to examine one's reactions to different clients.

The counselor needs to be able to effectively network with other service providers because many dual diagnosis clients have multiple psychosocial needs and problems. Crises often arise, so the counselor must also be conversant with crisis intervention approaches. An ability to work with a team is also essential in all treatment contexts.

Experience with addicts and mental health clients is the ideal. However, if a counselor is trained in one field and has access to additional training and supervision in the other, it is possible to expand knowledge and skills and work effectively with dual diagnosed clients.

Counselor's Recovery Status

If a counselor has the training, knowledge, and experiential background in working with psychiatric clients as well as addicts, a personal history of recovery can be helpful. Although self-disclosure is sometimes appropriate, in general the counselor providing treatment shares less of his/her own recovery experience than typically is shared in the more traditional Addiction Counseling model.

Ideal Personal Characteristics of Counselor

Helpful attitudes and characteristics of counselors include: hope and optimism for recovery, a high degree of empathy, patience, and tolerance, flexibility, an ability to enjoy working with difficult clients, a realistic perspective on change and steps toward success, a low need to control the client, an ability to engage the client yet be able to detach, and an ability to utilize a multiplicity of treatment interventions rather than relying on a single way of counseling.

Counselor's Behaviors

The DDRC approach involves a broad range of behaviors and interventions on the part of the counselor. Specific behaviors are mediated by the severity of the client's symptoms, his/her related needs and problems, and the treatment contract. The counselor's interventions may include any of the following:

- Providing information and education
- Providing support and encouragement
- Challenging denial and self-destructive behaviors. Confrontation is modified to take into account the client's ego strength and ability to tolerate confrontation
- Providing realistic feedback on problems and progress in treatment
- Encouraging and monitoring abstinence from alcohol, illicit drugs and non-prescribed drugs
- Helping the client get involved in self-help groups
- Helping the client to identify, prioritize, and work on problems and recovery issues that he/she identifies as important
- Monitoring addiction recovery issues (cravings, close calls, people, places and things, and high-risk relapse factors)
- Monitoring target psychiatric symptoms (suicidality, mood symptoms, thought disorder symptoms, or problem behaviors)

32

- Helping the client develop specific recovery skills (e.g., coping with drug or alcohol cravings, refusing offers to get high, challenging faulty thinking, coping with negative effect, improving interpersonal behaviors, managing relapse warning signs, etc.)
- Developing relapse prevention strategies
- Facilitating inpatient admissions when needed
- Failitating the use of community resources or services
- Advocating on behalf of the client
- Developing therapeutic assignments aimed at helping the client reach a goal or make a specific change
- Following up when a client fails to follow through with treatment in order to offer support, crisis intervention, and outreach

Counselor's Behaviors Contraindicated

The DDRC counselor does not typically interpret the client's behaviors or motivation. The focus is more on understanding and coping with practical issues related to the dual disorders and current functioning. The counselor avoids extensive exploration of past traumas during the early phase of recovery because this can lead to avoidance of addressing the substance use disorder and it can increase the client's anxiety. The DDRC counselor should also minimize time spent on co-dependency issues, because this also can deflect from the substance use problem and raises anxiety.

Harsh confrontation is avoided because this can adversely impact on the client's sense of self and drive the client away from treatment. Confrontation is used, but it should be done in a caring, nonjudgmental, nonpunitive, and reality-oriented manner.

33

CHAPTER FIVE

Supervision

Goals of Supervision

Supervision is important for several reasons. It provides counselors with an opportunity to develop and improve knowledge and skills related to working with dual disordered clients. Supervision provides a mechanism for counselors to address their own clinical concerns as well as personal reactions to certain types of clients, thus allowing them to work through attitudes, feelings, or behaviors that impede the counseling process. Supervision also provides a mechanism for accountability so that the counselor's work can be monitored for "quality of care" as well as for other administrative reasons such as to ensure productivity requirements are being met. The specific goals of supervision are to help the counselor:

- increase knowledge of dual disorders and the counseling process;
- improve specific counseling skills (e.g., setting an agenda, helping client develop new coping skills, etc.);
- deal with personal issues or reactions that impede therapeutic alliance or progress (e.g., anger toward a client who relapses, negative reactions to a client with a personality disorder, etc.);
- use personal strengths in the counseling process (e.g., use of own experiences, use of humor, etc.);
- maintain a reasonable therapeutic focus on the client's addiction and mental health disorder; and
- figure out strategies to work through impasses in counseling.

Formats for Supervision

A variety of formats can be used for supervision. The less knowledgeable and experienced a counselor is, the more extensive the supervision should be. Supervision should not focus solely on routine review of cases but more in-depth discussions of difficult clinical cases or areas the counselor wants to improve. Formats that can be used in supervision include the following:

- Discussion of individual counseling cases, family sessions, or group treatment sessions
- Review of written assessments, clinical notes, and treatment plans
- Live observation of counseling sessions
- Review and discussion of audiotapes or videotapes of counseling sessions
- Conducting co-therapy sessions
- Group supervision with other counselors in which individual, family, or groups are reviewed, and in which clinical concerns of mutual interest are shared and explored

The most helpful, but time-intensive formats are those in which the counselor can be "seen in action." This provides tremendous opportunities to identify personal or professional areas needing further attention. This is especially helpful for less experienced counselors. Once a counselor works through anxiety about being scrutinized in vivo or on tape, he/she usually finds this process helpful for professional development.

Counselors should receive specific feedback regarding their counseling. This includes positive reinforcement for good work as well as critical feedback on areas of weakness. For example, a group counselor can benefit from feedback pointing out that he/she talks too much in the group sessions, or tells clients how to cope with a recovery issue before eliciting their ideas on coping strategies. Similarly, counselors need to hear positive feedback on things they have done well in treatment sessions.

Use of Adherence Scales

The use of adherence scales, used in some clinical research protocols, is an excellent way of providing feedback on a specific treatment session. The counselor is rated on performing specific interventions as well as the quality of these interventions. The major drawback is that tapes of specific treatment sessions have to be reviewed in detail, a process requiring considerable time. This process could be especially helpful to newer, less experienced counselors although all clinicians can benefit from feedback regarding their work.

Following are sample adherence scales that can be used in rating individual and group treatment sessions. These scales are modeled after ones that we are using in a clinical research project for the treatment of cocaine addiction.[43]

Adherence Scale for Dual Disorders Recovery Counseling
Individual Treatment Sessions

Counselor: _____ Rater: _____

Session Date: _____ Date Rated: _____

Date Reviewed with Counselor: _____

Rate the quality of the counselor's interventions (i.e., how helpful and appropriate were the counselor's interventions during the session) using the 7-point rating scale below. Mark your rating in the blank to the immediate left of each item.

1	2	3	4	5	6	7
Not at All		Some		Considerably		Very Much

Quality   **Supporting Recovery and Motivating Client**

_____   1. Encouraging client to set an agenda for each counseling session.

_____   2. Encouraging client to discuss both the psychiatric and substance use problems.

_____   3. Encouraging client to discuss close calls and cravings for drugs or alcohol, and ways to manage them.

_____   4. Encouraging client to accept abstinence from alcohol, street drugs, and nonprescribed medications as a recovery goal.

_____   5. Encouraging client to focus on problem solving and identifying positive coping strategies related to specific issues or problems discussed.

_____   6. Encouraging client to discuss any substance use or significant change in psychiatric symptoms.

_____   7. Limiting discussions in counseling sessions to only one or two problem areas.

_____   8. Assigning therapeutic tasks to be completed between treatment sessions (e.g., completion of workbook activity, reading chapter of AA Big Book, NA Basic Text, Dual Recovery Book, etc.).

_____   9. Reviewing completed assignments in treatment sessions. If client fails to complete an assignment, discussing the reasons.

Quality　　　　　　　**Providing Feedback and Confrontation**

_____　　1. Confronting denial of client.

_____　　2. Pointing out self-defeating behaviors on the part of the client.

_____　　3. Helping client discuss the adverse effects of self-defeating behaviors, both on self and others.

_____　　4. Pointing out strengths of client and providing reinforcement for positive behaviors and coping strategies used.

_____　　5. Helping the client understand the connection between thoughts, feelings, and behaviors.

Providing Information and Education

_____　　1. Educating client about psychiatric illness, addiction, and relationship between dual disorders.

_____　　2. Helping client relate to educational material in a personal way (e.g., when discussing relapse warning signs, have client give personal examples of warning signs).

_____　　3. Educating client about treatments for dual disorders (professional therapies, medications, and self-help programs).

_____　　4. Providing client with information on specific issues or problems pertinent to his/her situation (e.g., information on depression, anger, NA, relapse, family issues in recovery, antidepressant medications, etc.).

Encouraging Participation in Self-Help Programs

_____　　1. Encouraging participation in 12-Step groups, mental health support groups, and/or dual recovery groups.

_____　　2. Expressing positive opinions about support groups.

_____　　3. Encouraging client to get and use an NA/AA/CA sponsor for help and support during recovery.

_____　　4. Discussing resistances or negative views that client has regarding self-help programs or sponsors.

Quality   **Discharge Planning (for Inpatients)**

_____ 1. Encouraging client to participate in ongoing professional treatment (partial hospital program, outpatient therapy, etc.).

_____ 2. Helping client identify positive aspects of continued involvement in follow-up.

_____ 3. Encouraging client to participate in self-help programs, use a sponsor, and get a home group.

_____ 4. Helping client identify specific problems and treatment issues to focus on in ongoing outpatient treatment.

_____ 5. Helping client understand the connection between ongoing involvement in therapy and self-help programs and positive treatment outcome.

_____ 6. Helping client develop an "emergency plan" to deal with unexpected setbacks or relapses to psychiatric illness, addiction, or both disorders.

Adherence Scale for Dual Disorders Recovery Counseling Group Treatment Sessions

Counselor: _____   Rater: _____

Type of Group: _____ Psychoeducational _____ Problem Solving _____ Therapy

Session Number (for Psychoeducational Group Only): _____

Session Date: _____   Date Rated: _____

Date Reviewed with Counselor: _____

Rate the quality of the counselor's interventions (i.e., how helpful and appropriate were the counselor's interventions during the group session) using the 7-point rating scale below. Mark your rating in the blank to the immediate left of each item.

1	2	3	4	5	6	7
Not at All		Some		Considerably		Very Much

Quality   **Supporting Recovery and Motivating Client**

_____ 1. Encouraging clients to discuss both the psychiatric and substance-use problems.

_____ 2. Encouraging clients to discuss cravings for drugs/alcohol or "close calls."

_____ 3. Encouraging clients to discuss any episodes of actual substance use and strategies to stop use.

_____ 4. Encouraging clients to accept abstinence from alcohol, street drugs, and non-prescribed medications as a recovery goal.

_____ 5. Encouraging clients to discuss both behavioral and cognitive coping strategies related to specific recovery issues or problems discussed.

_____ 6. Encouraging clients to discuss psychiatric problems and coping strategies.

Quality   **Providing Feedback and Confrontation**

_____ 1. Confronting the denial of a client or encouraging other group members to do so.

_____ 2. Pointing out self-defeating behaviors of clients or encouraging other group members to do so.

_____ 3. Helping clients discuss the adverse effects of self-defeating behaviors, both on self and others.

_____ 4. Pointing out strengths of clients and providing reinforcement for positive behaviors or coping strategies used.

_____ 5. Helping clients understand the connection between thoughts, feelings, and behaviors.

Providing Information and Education

_____ 1. Educating clients about psychiatric illness, addiction, and relationships between dual disorders.

_____ 2. Helping clients relate to psychoeducational material in a personal way.

_____ 3. Educating clients about treatments for dual disorders (professional therapies, medications, and self-help programs).

_____ 4. Educating clients about role of medication in recovery from psychiatric illness, and effects of using alcohol or drugs on efficacy of medications.

_____ 5. Providing clients with information on specific issues or problems pertinent to their situation (e.g., information on depression, anger, AA or NA, relapse, family issues in recovery, antidepressant medications, etc.).

Encouraging Participation in Self-Help Programs

_____ 1. Encouraging participation in 12-Step groups, mental health support groups, and/or dual recovery groups.

_____ 2. Expressing positive opinions about support groups.

_____ 3. Encouraging clients to get and use an NA/AA/CA/DRA sponsor.

_____ 4. Discussing resistances or negative views that clients have regarding self-help programs or sponsors.

Quality	**Facilitating Group Participation**
_____	1. Encouraging all clients to participate in group discussions.
_____	2. Encouraging clients to give each other constructive feedback.
_____	3. Encouraging clients to be specific when discussing strategies to cope with recovery issues or problems related to either disorder.
_____	4. Encouraging clients to discuss recovery plans they will follow between group sessions.
_____	5. Ensuring that one or two clients do not dominate the entire group discussion so that all members talk in the session.

For Psychoeducational Groups

_____	1. Educating clients on group topic by reviewing major points identified in the session outline.
_____	2. Encouraging clients to relate to psychoeducational material by sharing personal experiences or reactions.
_____	3. Facilitating discussion among clients of their responses to the group session psychoeducational material.
_____	4. Keeping discussions focused on the session topic.

For Problem-Solving Groups

_____	1. Helping clients identify and prioritize specific concerns and problems to discuss in the group session.
_____	2. Facilitating discussion among clients of various problems and concerns presented.
_____	3. Helping clients identify and discuss strategies to cope with the various problems or concerns identified (ensuring that adequate time is spent on coping strategies, not just discussion of problems).
_____	4. Keeping discussions focused on problems and concerns raised by clients in the group.

CHAPTER SIX
Client/Counselor Relationship

Counselor's Role

As evidenced by the list of counselor behaviors in chapter four, many roles are assumed in DDRC: educator, collaborator, adviser, advocate, and problem solver.

Who Talks More?

Although the counselor is very active asking questions, clarifying problems and feelings, and leading the client to identify ways to cope with problems, usually the client talks the most during individual DDRC sessions. In psychoeducational groups the counselor is very active in providing education to the group. However, clients are encouraged to ask questions, share personal experiences related to the group topic, and express their ideas on ways to cope with problems or recovery issues reviewed during the group session. In therapy or problem-solving groups, the group leader is less active verbally than in psychoeducational groups.

Directiveness of Counselor

In DDRC the counselor may be very directive and active with one client, and less directive and active with another. The approach must be individualized and take into account each client's strengths, abilities, deficits, and response to feedback. However, the counselor is generally more directive than in traditional mental health counseling, particularly in relation to continued substance use, relapse set-ups, pointing out self-defeating behavior patterns, recommending support group meetings, and pointing out concrete strategies for handling alcohol or drug cravings, pressures to use chemicals, or ways to deal with negative effect or interpersonal conflict. Direct advice, however, is usually given after eliciting the client's ideas on coping strategies for particular problems.

Therapeutic Alliance (TA)

A good TA facilitates recovery[46,47] and is based on the counselor's ability to "connect with the client," respect differences, show empathy, use humor, and understand the "inner world" of the client. Listening; providing information; being supportive, encouraging, and humorous; and being up front and directive can help build the TA.

A poor TA often shows in missed appointments or failure to comply with treatment. Discussing common problems in recovery and acknowledging specific problems between the counselor and client can help improve a poor alliance. Calling clients who drop out of treatment early and inquiring as to whether they think a new treatment plan can help may help correct a poor TA. Discussion of specific cases in supervision can help the counselor identify causes of a poor TA as well as strategies to correct it. As a last resort, a case may be transferred to another counselor if the client/counselor relationship is such that a TA cannot be formed.

CHAPTER SEVEN
The Assessment Process

Components of Assessment

The *initial assessment* involves a combination of the following: psychiatric evaluation, mental status exam, addiction history, physical examination, laboratory work, and urinalysis. Client and collateral interviews and review of previous records can be part of the assessment process. The assessment process for inpatient treatment is more extensive and involved than assessment for outpatient care.

Ongoing assessment involves monitoring psychiatric symptoms and substance use. Questions asked during counseling sessions, discussions with family or other service providers, completion of rating scales, blood work (for patients on certain medications), urine drug screens, and breathalyzer tests can be used to continuously assess the client.

Areas on which to Gather Information

An assessment gathers information on the following areas: current problems, symptoms and reasons for referral, current and past psychiatric history, current and past substance use and abuse, history of treatment, mental status, medical history, family history, developmental history (childhood development, school, work, etc.), current stressors, social support system, current and past suicidality, current and past aggressiveness or homicidality, and other areas based on the judgment of the evaluation team (e.g., relapse history, patterns of hospitalization, etc.). Clinical diagnoses are formulated based on criteria for disorders as outlined in DSM-IV.[48]

Substance Abuse History

The substance abuse history should include specific substances used (currently and in the past), patterns of use (frequency, quantity, methods), context of use, and consequence of use (medical, psychiatric, family, legal, occupational, spiritual, financial). It should also include review of substance abuse or dependency symptoms such as loss of control, obsession or preoccupation, tolerance changes, inability to abstain despite repeated attempts, withdrawal syndromes, continuation of use despite psychosocial problems, and impairment caused by intoxications. Clinical interviews can be used as well as specific assessment instruments such as the Addiction Severity Index (ASI),[49] Drug Use Screening Inventory (DUSI),[50] Drug Abuse Screening Test (DAST),[51] Michigan Alcoholism Screening Test (MAST),[52] or other addiction specific instruments.[53,54] Regular or random urinalysis and/or breathalyzers can be used to monitor substance use, particularly in the early phases of recovery.

43

Assessment Instruments

Specific instruments may also be used for psychiatric disorders in order to get objective and subjective data. These may be administered by a professional (e.g., SCID[55,56] or certain personality disorder interviews). Or, they may be completed by the client at different points in time (e.g., Beck[57,58] or Hamilton Depression[59,60] or anxiety inventories, mania scales[61] or other scales at intake and at regular intervals). These can be used to gather baseline data as well as to measure change in symptoms over time.

Workbook Assignments

Review of recovery workbook assignments or the "Substance Abuse Problem Checklist"[62] are also useful in assessing the client's problems, ability to develop recovery plans, or motivation to comply with treatment. These tools can be used by the counselor to identify specific areas to focus on in individual DDRC sessions.

Quality Assurance/Quality Improvement

Assessing clients periodically can be a helpful quality assurance and quality improvement (QA/QI) activity. This process provides important information on specific clients regarding how they function or change over time. QA/QI data compiled on a clinic's client population gives very important information on a variety of important issues such as:

- Overall compliance rates with scheduled appointments by clients
- Changes in substance use patterns of clients
- Change in psychiatric symptom of clients
- Patterns of compliance with treatment plans, including the use of medications
- Hospitalization rates
- Client use of support groups
- Client use of other services (vocational, social service, etc.)
- Rates of treatment completion
- Client or family satisfaction with services

44

CHAPTER EIGHT
Individual Treatment

Length of Treatment

In acute care and time-limited inpatient settings, most clients stay between several days and weeks. Therefore, a limited number of individual sessions are available to the individual counselor. The fewer individual treatment sessions available, the more limited and focused the direction of treatment will be.

In partial hospital and outpatient settings, the length of treatment may vary considerably, depending on the client's problems, the therapist's treatment philosophy, and the source of reimbursement. When the client first enters treatment, it is helpful to establish an initial, time-limited contract with the understanding that this contract can be reevaluated and changed as needed, based on the client's progress and symptom change over time. We often use a three-month initial contract. A treatment contract sets the expectation that treatment does not last indefinitely (although chronically ill clients may go in and out of treatment over a very long period of time). Many counselors are used to providing long-term treatment in order to help clients explore important issues relevant to their disorders. However, because managed care limits the number of sessions a clinician can provide, shorter-term contracts are being used more frequently than in the past.

Typical Individual Session

An individual DDRC session reviews addiction and mental health recovery issues. The time spent in a given session on addiction or mental health issues varies and depends on the specific issues and recovery status of a given client. For example, even if a depressed alcoholic client were sober nine months, the counselor may briefly inquire about any number of addiction recovery issues (e.g., cravings or close calls, involvement in self-help group meetings, discussions with sponsors, etc.). Or, if an addicted client's depression were improved, the counselor would inquire about the typical symptoms this client had before coming to treatment (mood, suicidality, energy, etc.). Any crisis issues would be attended to as well.

Some clients will exhibit very low motivation to address the substance use problem and prefer working only on the psychiatric disorder. It may take time for the counselor to develop a solid therapeutic relationship and be able to influence the client to also focus on substance use issues. Great patience and flexibility are needed in such cases.

The majority of the time of the individual counseling session focuses on the client's agenda unless a crisis takes up the session. The client is usually asked at the beginning of the session, "What concern or problem do you want to focus on in today's session?" The problem or concern should be one the client has identified as an important part of his/her treatment plan. In relation to the problem or issues identified, the counselor helps the client to explore this to better understand and cope with it. Coping strategies are especially important because the session should be a purposeful one aimed at helping the client work toward awareness and change. During the course of the DDRC session, any "live" material that is relevant to the client's dual disorders or recovery can be processed. For example, if the client gives evidence of "maladaptive thinking" in the session contributing to anxiety or depressive symptoms such as "jumping to conclusions" or "focusing only on the negative," this can be pointed out and discussed in the context of the client's problems. Or, if the client becomes frustrated and angry at the counselor in a session or on the telephone because the counselor cannot meet his/her unrealistic expectations or demands, the counselor can discuss this interaction to help the client understand how such attitudes and expectations impact on interpersonal relationships.

It is helpful for the counselor to provide encouragement and positive feedback at the end of the session for the work the client accomplished or for the effort put forth. Frequently clients have difficulty seeing progress or acknowledging efforts at changing. Expectations are often high and unrealistic, and positive changes—especially small changes, are ignored and minimized by clients. Feedback from the counselor helps counteract this and provides the client with a more realistic view of the recovery process.

The DDRC session ends with a review of what the client will be doing between this and the next session relating to his/her recovery. Reading, writing, or behavioral assignments may be given at the end of the session. These therapeutic assignments aim to get the client to actively work on problems and issues between counseling sessions. For example, a client who has a serious problem expressing anger impulsively and inappropriately can be asked to keep a "daily anger log." This anger log is used to record situations triggering anger, the degree to which anger is experienced, thoughts, actual actions taken, and new ideas on positive coping strategies. This log can then be reviewed during each treatment session to further explore strategies to help the client deal with the problem of coping with anger. Or, a client who is lonely, isolated, and depressed may be given the assigned task of initiating a social contact with one friend. A therapeutic assignment can be developed with the client and should not be too difficult to achieve. Assignments that have some degree of difficulty provide the client with an opportunity for mastery over problems.

Recovery Themes at Various Phases of Treatment

The recovery themes that follow can be reviewed in individual sessions. Specific areas of focus will depend on the client's current problems and needs, where he/she is in the recovery process, and the specific treatment contract. Short-term treatment (less than 12 sessions), for example, would be limited to just a few of these key themes. Following is a brief listing of the themes associated with each phase of recovery. Although separated for purposes of discussion, there is overlap among these various themes. Not all themes can be explored in treatment. Clients involved in ongoing self-help groups can continue focusing on recovery issues over time.

Phase 1: Transition and Engagement

a. Discuss specific symptoms and problems leading client to treatment.
b. Help client understand the specific diagnoses (both psychiatric and addictive illness) and accept the reality of the dual disorders.
c. Discuss disorders as "no fault" biopsychosocial disorders or diseases with multiple causes and effects on the client and family.

46

d. Help client recognize an inability to consistently control the use of alcohol or other drugs.

e. Discuss the effects of substance use on psychiatric symptoms (covering up, triggering off, or worsening psychiatric symptoms).

f. Discuss the client's thoughts and feelings about being in treatment, particularly if treatment is involuntary or resulted from pressure from an external source (family, employer, etc.).

g. Validate the client's ambivalence about treatment and recovery.

h. Help the client understand and accept the need for family involvement when indicated.

i. Discuss the role of medications in treatment, if relevant, and discuss the client's perception of taking medications.

Phase 2: Stabilization

a. Discuss the process of stabilizing from acute psychiatric symptoms and how treatment can help both short-term and long-term recovery.

b. Discuss the process of getting alcohol and drugs out of the system and adjusting to being chemically free.

c. Discuss what the client will miss about giving up alcohol or other drugs as well as the benefits of getting sober.

d. Provide additional information on addictive and psychiatric illnesses, and the role of professional therapy, medications, and self-help programs in ongoing recovery.

e. Continue to help the client accept the dual diagnoses.

f. Discuss the client's expectations regarding treatment.

g. Monitor cravings and "close calls," discuss common internal and external triggers to alcohol and drug cravings, and review strategies to cope with these.

h. Monitor major psychiatric symptoms and discuss strategies to cope with symptoms and problems associated with the psychiatric illness.

i. Discuss the benefits of getting involved in self-help programs and any resistances or negative perceptions the client has regarding support programs.

j. Help the client develop a problem list incorporating the psychiatric illness, the addiction, and related life problems to work on during recovery.

k. Continue to discuss the need for total abstinence from alcohol, street drugs, and nonprescribed drugs as the path to take in recovery.

l. Continue to discuss the importance of family involvement in treatment.

m. Monitor medication compliance and discuss any deviation from the medication regimen.

n. Monitor self-help group attendance and discuss any concerns the client has regarding support programs.

Phase 3: Early Recovery

a. Discuss strategies to avoid and/or cope with people, places, and things that represent a relapse risk for addiction.

b. Discuss nonchemical ways of coping with pressures from others to use alcohol or other drugs, and coping with situations that in the past led to using chemicals.

c. Discuss negative thinking and faulty beliefs associated with addiction or psychiatric illness.

d. Discuss the concept of "persistent symptoms" of psychiatric illness if relevant and discuss ways to cope with these.

e. Continue to monitor psychiatric symptoms, cravings, or close calls related to substance use, medication compliance, attendance at self-help groups, and discussions with a sponsor.

f. Help the client identify behaviors to change, especially ones that caused difficulties in the past, and strategies to make behavioral changes.

g. Discuss the importance of methods for building structure and regularity into day-to-day life to keep busy, stay focused on recovery issues, get involved in enjoyable leisure activities, and limit the amount of free time available.

h. Discuss the impact of the dual disorders and behaviors on the family and continue discussing ways to work with the family in recovery.

i. Discuss issues related to feelings of guilt and shame that are associated with psychiatric illness, addiction, or both.

j. Help client see progress, even in small changes.

k. Discuss any relapses or setbacks and help client learn from these.

Phase 4: Middle Recovery

a. Continue to get client to increase self-disclosure about inner thoughts, feelings and problems.

b. Discuss the process of making amends to family and other significant people hurt by behaviors.

c. Discuss other relationship problems.

d. Discuss ways for the client to improve communication and strengthen interpersonal relationships.

e. Discuss spirituality issues.

f. Continue discussing strategies to develop and/or improve cognitive and behavioral coping strategies to deal with negative or upsetting thoughts, feelings, and problems.

g. Help client identify warning signs of psychiatric relapse and strategies to manage these.

h. Help client identify warning signs of addiction lapse or relapse and strategies to manage these.

i. Discuss strategies the client can use to monitor recovery on a daily basis.

j. Continue to monitor psychiatric symptoms, cravings or close calls related to substance use, medication compliance, attendance at self-help groups, and discussions with a sponsor.

k. Discuss any relapses or setbacks and help client learn from these.

Phase 5: Late Recovery

a. Discuss ways to change character defects or personality traits that cause self-defeating behaviors or other problems.

b. Continue to help client increase awareness of "inner self" (defenses, personality traits, values, strengths, and vulnerabilities).

c. When relevant, help client gain a greater understanding of past influences on current behaviors, values, and relationships.

d. Deal more in depth with family-of-origin issues if needed in order to heal from past emotional pain.

e. Discuss the advantages of broadening support-group involvement if needed to include ACOA or survivor groups.

f. Focus more on "lifestyle balancing" so that attention is directed to all major areas of life—recovery, work, love, relationships, fun, and spirituality.

Phase 6: Maintenance

a. Discuss "giving away" what one learned in recovery by sponsoring others or serving the greater good of society.

b. Continue to monitor recovery from dual disorders and discuss any problems, concerns, or setbacks the client raises.

c. Continue discussions of ways to grow in recovery and change self and/or lifestyle.

d. Discuss any relapses or setbacks and help client learn from these.

Treatment Entry and Reengagement Strategies

Many clients who request treatment for dual disorders do not show up for their assessment or initial treatment appointment. In addition, many who are discharged from inpatient care fail to keep their treatment appointments for outpatient or partial hospital treatment, thus negating the gains made during inpatient hospitalization. Strategies to enhance treatment entry or reengagement, and increase motivation during the early phase of recovery, include:[63-78]

- Using motivational interviewing.

- Using prompts to remind the client about the initial treatment session(s) (e.g., phone calls and/or letters).

- Providing reinforcement for attending treatment sessions (e.g., tangible rewards such as bus tickets, vouchers that can be cashed in for merchandise, etc.).

- Giving quick appointments (less than one week from the time of referral; preferably see the client within two or three days of the initial call for treatment).

- Collaborating with inpatient referrals (for outpatient clinicians).

- Helping the client deal with other problems (e.g., transportation, child care, etc.) that often interfere with ability to attend treatment sessions.

- Intensive contact in the early weeks of treatment (e.g., seeing the client more than once per week, or providing individual and group treatment).
- Using intensive case managers or other specialty workers to provide outreach or help with other needs.
- Making quick contact with clients who fail to show for appointments to offer another appointment (e.g., making phone calls or sending letters within 24–48 hours of the missed appointment).

Typical Treatment Team Session

Medication visits and special psychiatric consultations are ideally held with the counselor and psychiatrist together. This ensures integrated care, helps prevent the client from "splitting" the counselor and psychiatrist, and enhances ongoing team communication. These visits are usually brief and focus on medication, treatment compliance, or emergency psychiatric issues. The counselor gives the psychiatrist an update on treatment before the joint meeting. The counselor adds input during the session as needed. The psychiatrist and counselor can strategize after the session regarding changes in therapeutic interventions.

The counselor can also consult with the team psychiatrist between sessions as needed to address significant changes in symptomology, side effects of medication, or possible need for inpatient hospitalization.

Strategies for Dealing with Common Clinical Problems

Lateness is discussed directly with the client to determine the reasons for it and strategies for better compliance with treatment sessions. Chronic patterns of lateness may be generalized as indicative of broader patterns of difficulty with responsibility or as part of a self-defeating pattern of behavior.

Missed sessions are discussed to determine the reasons and to work through any resistances on the part of the client. Clients who fail to show or call for appointments are usually called by the clinician, or a friendly note is sent in the mail offering another appointment or asking the client to call so that another appointment can be set. This makes it easier for the client to reengage in treatment sessions.

Interventions with clients who come to sessions under the influence are dealt with in a variety of ways, depending on their condition. Detoxification and inpatient hospitalization may be arranged in severe cases involving potential withdrawal and florid psychiatric symptoms which cannot be managed on an outpatient basis (e.g., severe mood or thought disorder symptoms that interfere with the client's ability to function, suicidal attempts or plans, or homicidal attempts or plans). In other cases, crisis intervention may be provided, or the client may be helped to make arrangements to go home and return for another appointment when not under the influence of chemicals. Generally these situations are dealt with in the most appropriate clinical manner. Limits can be set without coming across as punitive or judgmental.

Noncompliance with medication (taking more or less than prescribed) is dealt with by discussing the client's reasons for not taking the medication as prescribed and discussing the actual or potential effects of this on symptoms and recovery. Uncomfortable side effects or difficulty following a medication regimen involving several medications or having to take multiple doses per day are common reasons for less than 100-percent compliance with medicine.

If a client does not complete a therapeutic assignment (e.g., behavioral task, reading or writing assignment), the counselor should discuss the reason for this and try to figure out whether or not the assignment was too difficult. If the client relates the task was too difficult, a simpler task can be given. If the client forgets or has some other excuse for not completing the assignment, this can be explored further in the session to determine why the client has been unable or unwilling to follow through with the assignment.

Some clients constantly want to change the focus of therapy (within or between individual treatment sessions) based on an endless number of concerns or life crises that constantly pop up. While some focus on crises is inevitable, the counselor should avoid non-focused treatment and try to keep to the structure of therapy by focusing on issues identified. This requires checking out why the client wants to change the focus of the session. Such change of focus may represent avoidance or may be the client's way of saying that he/she is anxious about or not ready to explore a specific issue in treatment.

Specific contracts can be devised with particular clients around lateness, missed sessions, failure to take medications as prescribed or attend medication visits in order to get refills, failure to complete therapeutic assignments, or coming to sessions under the influence of chemicals. Clients can give their input on how these situations should be dealt with by the counselor or treatment team.

Strategies for Dealing with Denial, Resistance, or Poor Motivation

Treatment sessions deal with clients' ambivalence regarding ongoing participation in treatment as the need arises. The counselor attempts to normalize and validate ambivalence or denial in the context of addiction and/or psychiatric illness. Education, support, the use of therapeutic assignments, sessions with the treatment team to discuss symptoms and behaviors of the client, and sessions involving the family or significant others may be used to help deal with denial and resistance. Generally any resistance is "grist for the therapeutic mill" and is explored in treatment sessions.

Poor motivation is usually seen as a manifestation of illness, particularly with more severely addicted or psychiatrically impaired clients. Personality issues also greatly contribute to resistance and poor motivation. The "door is usually left open" so poorly motivated clients can reenter treatment easily. However, limits can still be set by the treatment team so the client knows that misusing treatment will not be tolerated. For example, clients who miss counseling appointments and medication visits and then call the counselor in a crisis when medications have run out may be given a physician's prescription for a week with the caveat that future refills are contingent on better participation in treatment sessions. The client is then given an appointment. Clients who have not been seen for months or longer usually should not be given medication refills unless first seen by the treatment team.

Strategies for Dealing with Crises

A very flexible approach is needed to dealing with crises because dual diagnosis clients often experience exacerbations of either illness. In more severe cases, voluntary or involuntary hospitalization may be pursued to help stabilize a client in a severe psychiatric crisis. Extra face-to-face sessions with any member(s) of the treatment team, including the case manager for persistently

51

mentally ill clients, may also be held. In some instances supportive sessions via telephone are held. Clients are given an emergency phone number that can be called 24 hours a day, seven days per week, and are instructed on how and when to use the Psychiatric Emergency Room.

Substance Use Lapses and Relapses; Recurrence of Psychiatric Symptoms

The counselor typically approaches substance use lapses or relapses as opportunities for the client to learn about relapse precipitants or set-ups. All lapses and relapses to substance use are explored in an attempt to identify warning signs that preceded them. Strategies are discussed to help the client better prepare for recovery in the future. Extra sessions or telephone contacts may be used to help the client stabilize from some relapses. Inpatient detoxification or rehabilitation programs may be arranged in instances where the relapse is severe and cannot be interrupted with the help and support of counseling along with self-help programs such as AA, NA, or CA.

Substance use relapses are processed in terms of their impact on psychiatric symptoms and recovery from dual disorders. If a client is on medication, the possible interactions with alcohol or nonprescribed drugs are discussed.

Psychiatric recurrences are discussed in terms of warning signs and causes in order to help the client figure out what may have contributed to the return of symptoms. Extra sessions with the counselor or other members of the treatment team (or even telephone calls) may be provided to help the client stabilize. Medication adjustments may also be made, depending on the symptoms experienced by the client.

When psychiatric symptoms are life-threatening or cause significant impairment in functioning, an inpatient hospitalization is arranged. The counselor helps to orchestrate an involuntary commitment if needed in severe cases where a client's welfare (or that of another person) is in jeopardy and the client refuses to enter the hospital voluntarily.

In any of these or similar cases, the counselor assumes a helpful, supportive, and nonjudgmental stance. He/she also does not personalize episodes of relapse or other setbacks and accepts these as part of working with dual diagnosed clients.

52

CHAPTER NINE
Role of the Family and Significant Others in Treatment

Effects of Dual Disorders on the Family System and Individual Members

The family unit as well as individual family members and significant others are often adversely affected by the client's behaviors associated with the psychiatric illness, addiction, or both.[2] The family system is often disrupted and any area of family life can be affected such as communication, interactions, emotional health, and financial condition. With good intentions, the family may show enabling behaviors that help perpetuate the problems. Enabling may be *passive* in which the family does nothing and accepts problematic behaviors related to the substance use or psychiatric disorder of the ill family member. Or, enabling may be *active* in which the family covers up the problems caused by the dual disordered member. Sometimes this involves bailing the ill member out of legal, financial, or other types of trouble, or assuming his or her responsibility.

Dual disorders often takes an emotional toll on individual family members — parents, spouses, children, siblings, and other relatives. Stress can be very high and, as a result of exposure to intoxicated, violent, erratic, or unpredictable behaviors, family members feel upset, angry, confused, anxious, worried, or depressed. Some family members, especially parents, even feel guilty and responsible for causing the dual disordered member's problems.

Children can be affected by dual disorders and may have emotional, behavioral, academic, or substance abuse problems themselves as a direct or indirect result of exposure to a parent's disorders over time. They need education, support, and an opportunity to share some of their worries, feelings, and concerns. Children with serious problems need treatment themselves.

Goals of Family Involvement

Involving the family in the assessment and treatment processes is helpful in several respects. Family participation:

- Allows the counselor to gather important information from the family regarding how they view and relate to the dual disordered family member, and the effects of the illness on the family.
- Gives the counselor an idea on the strengths of the family and how they might be able to support the dual disordered member's recovery.
- Provides an opportunity to figure out how the family and client get along, and how the family affects the client's functioning.
- Provides the family with an opportunity to gain information, support, and help with their own feelings and issues.
- Helps the counselor determine if other family members may need an evaluation or treatment for a serious emotional, behavioral, or substance use problem (e.g., a child of a client).

53

Typical Concerns of Family Members

There are a number of questions and concerns that are commonly expressed by family members of dual disordered clients. Awareness of these concerns can aid the counselor in working with the family. These questions and concerns include, but are not limited to, the following:[2]

1. Specific diagnoses and the implications of these.

2. Causes of the dual disorders.

3. Treatment recommendations, length of time in treatment, expected outcome of treatment interventions, and cost of treatment.

4. Medications, side effects, and interactions with alcohol, street drugs, or nonprescribed drugs.

5. Family role in treatment in relation to supporting the dual disordered family member's recovery.

6. Family role in treatment in relation to their own needs, problems, and concerns.

7. How to deal with frightening behavior (violence or the threat of it; suicidal action or the threat of it; psychotic, manic, or severe anxiety or depression).

8. Whether or not other family members are vulnerable to psychiatric illness, substance abuse, or both—especially offspring.

9. Whether or not the ill family member will be able to function at a job, school, or home.

10. How to deal with emotional reactions toward the dual disordered family member (e.g., anger, disappointment, worry, etc.).

11. How to deal with a dual disordered family member who refuses to get help or comply with treatment.

12. How to deal with psychiatric relapse.

13. How to deal with alcohol or drug addiction relapse.

14. When detoxification or psychiatric hospitalization are needed.

Types of Family Treatment

There are a variety of different family treatments that can be used, depending on the client's situation and the availability of services in a clinic or program. These include the following:

- Psychoeducational (PE) programs that provide information regarding dual disorders and recovery and ways the family can cope with their concerns regarding the ill family member. These usually are offered to several families together and can be held regularly such as once per week for a specified length of time, on a periodic basis such as monthly, bi-monthly, half-day, or full-day family PE workshops, or as a "one-shot" deal such as a famly PE workshop.

- Family therapy in which issues and problems within a specific family of a dual diagnosed client are explored from a family systems perspective.

- Couples therapy or parent/child therapy in which specific problems between a dyad are explored.

- Multiple family groups that combine psychoeducation, support, and discussion of mutual problems and concerns of families.

- Exposure to family support groups for addiction such as Al-Anon, Naranon, Alateen, Alatots, Parents groups, or Codependency Anonymous.

- Exposure to family support groups for mental illness such as NAMI (National Alliance of the Mentally Ill) groups.

Family involvement will not always be possible. Some clients are disengaged from their families and have no one whom they can involve in treatment. Some families will not want to get involved in treatment at all, especially if they have had numerous previous involvements. They may be tired, worn out, or burned out.

Family resistance to treatment or client resistance to family involvement in treatment should not be taken at face value as there are strategies that can be used to engage the family in treatment. Patience, persistence, and creativity are often needed on the part of the counselor to engage the family in sessions.

Principles of Family Treatment

A professional does not have to be a family therapist to help a family. The following principles can help guide the counselor and treatment team in working with families.

1. Don't label the family as sick, dysfunctional, or codependent. View them as allies in the treatment process, not as "the client."

2. Establish contact with the family as early as possible in the assessment and treatment processes.

3. View the engagement process as just as important as the educational and treatment processes. If a family cannot be engaged in treatment, the best treatment available will not mean anything.

4. Be patient and flexible with families. Use outreach phone calls as needed and ask families for help in understanding and working with the client. Don't rely on the client to invite the family to sessions if it is fairly certain that the client will resist this or sabotage the chances of the family showing up for sessions.

5. Be accessible to families. Offer evening appointments if convenient for the family. Be available to talk by telephone as needed.

6. Focus on family strengths. Don't overemphasize family deficits or problems at the expense of overlooking their strengths.

7. Provide a framework for the family to understand what is happening to the client and family system. Educating the family about mental illness, addiction, the course of illness, and recovery is an excellent way to provide this framework. Use the no-fault, biopsychosocial disease approach.

8. **Connect with the family emotionally** by letting them know you can understand their feelings, concerns, and worries. Give them ample opportunity to vent their frustrations and feelings. This will make it easier to later help them explore ways of coping with these feelings and adapting to the dual disordered member's recovery.

9. **Provide hope** by discussing how treatment benefits dual diagnosis clients and their families.

10. **Provide a realistic view on treatment and recovery.** Prepare them for the possibility of setbacks and relapses. If relevant, discuss issues around involuntary commitment in cases where the ill member is at risk for suicide or homicide, or if functioning has decompensated severely and the client is unable to take care of basic needs.

11. **Link the family with family support groups** in the community.

12. **Link the family with other resources** in the community as needed for the client (e.g., social services agencies, housing agencies, etc.).

CHAPTER TEN
Overview of Group Treatments

Goals of Group Treatment

Group treatment is a vital part of recovery for many clients with dual disorders. There are a variety of group treatments that provide clients a mechanism in which to explore common problems and concerns and learn recovery skills. Issues or problems discussed in group sessions can also be explored in individual treatment sessions. Conversely, issues or problems identified in individual sessions may be explored or worked on in the context of various treatment group sessions.

Overall, group treatment aims to provide a balance between focusing on the psychiatric and the chemical dependency disorders. However, a specific group session may focus mainly on one of these areas although the interrelationship between the disorders is continuously emphasized when appropriate.

Even though each type of group treatment has a particular format and objectives, the overall goals of group treatments are:

1. *Education*: Provide information on psychiatric illness, alcohol and drug addiction, and recovery from dual disorders.

2. *Self-awareness*: Increase the client's self-awareness so that he/she can relate to the material in a personal way and become aware of specific issues or problems needing addressed in treatment.

3. *Motivation*: Help the client to develop motivation to change and accept the need for involvement in ongoing professional treatment and self-help programs (e.g., AA, NA, DRA, or mental health support groups).

4. *Change*: Facilitate change in the client's attitudes, behaviors, and coping skills.

5. *Skill development*: Help the client develop skills to solve problems and deal with recovery issues and related life problems. These include cognitive, behavioral, and life skills the client can use on an ongoing basis.

The amount of focus on each of these areas depends on the type of group treatment provided. For example, open-ended process or psychotherapy groups focus more on self-awareness and problem-solving strategies while psychoeducational and skill groups focus more on providing information and helping the client learn specific recovery skills such as ways to refuse pressures to use alcohol or drugs, cope with feelings of boredom, or how to improve relationships.

Types and Structure of Dual Recovery Groups

A variety of "types" of groups can be used with dual diagnosis clients. These include unstructured process or psychotherapy groups, creative and expressive therapy groups, structured coping skills and psychoeducational groups, stress management, client-led groups, family groups, and self-help groups.

Both the **content** and **process** are important aspects of groups. Content refers to the *what* of group (i.e., the topics, issues, problems, or skills reviewed in the group treatment sessions). Process refers to the *how* of group (i.e., the way the group is conducted and the clients interact). Open discussion of issues or problems of a specific group of clients, lectures, behavioral role-plays, monodramas, review of workbook and other written assignments, and the use of creative media are the more common ways problems or issues are explored in treatment group sessions. Group process issues such as group members' avoidance of emotionally charged issues or how group members interact can also be discussed.

Dual recovery treatment groups are interactive and aim to get clients actively involved in the group process by sharing their experiences, problems, and feelings, and practicing new ways of coping with problems. In many cases the process of helping clients share their problems and concerns, and learning to trust others or lean on them for help and support is therapeutic in and of itself.

Therapeutic assignments may be given during a group session or between group sessions. These include bibliotherapy, journals or logs, workbooks, or other assignments created by group leaders. Although groups can be conducted by one leader, when possible co-leaders are recommended.

The types of groups used will depend on the treatment setting and time available to provide services. Inpatient programs in acute care hospitals are typically short term, lasting less than three weeks. Partial hospital programs usually last six months to a year or longer. Outpatient programs are more variable, lasting from a few months to a year or longer. Obviously the longer time counselors have clients in treatment, the more extensive group programming can be provided. However, even in very time-limited clinical situations, it is possible to offer group treatments that address important dual recovery issues.

Dual recovery treatment groups fall into one of several categories. Following is a brief description of various group treatments that can be used with dual diagnosis clients. These group treatments can be adapted to inpatient, partial hospital, intensive outpatient, or outpatient settings. Group treatments can also be devised for various levels of functioning. For example, lower functioning clients can benefit from a specialized group that is concrete and limited in the focus. Clients will feel more comfortable and able to participate than they would in a group with much higher functioning clients who are more verbal, insightful, and able to interact.

Psychotherapy Group

Psychotherapy group, also referred to as "process group," is an unstructured group that provides clients with an opportunity to discuss their problems, concerns, and feelings. Clients must take responsibility in these groups in identifying specific problems or recovery issues to work on. A variety of intrapersonal and interpersonal issues can be addressed in these groups. The specific issues addressed will depend on the clients in a particular group.

These groups can be conducted with men and women together, or gender specific groups can be provided so that women have an opportunity to work with other women in therapy, and men have a chance to work with other men. Gender specific groups are very popular among clients in some of our dual diagnosis programs.

In addition to the problems or issues raised by clients for discussion, "process" issues can be discussed as they emerge during the course of the group session. Some examples include issues such as a group member's passivity, tendency to dominate, or tendency to not listen to others, conflicts between group members, or other interpersonal behaviors oberved in the group by the leader.

In inpatient, partial hospital, or intensive outpatient settings, this type of group treatment can be held up to five times per week for an hour to an hour and a half. In outpatient treatment, this type of group is usually held once per week for an hour and a half.

Creative and Expressive Therapy Groups

These groups provide clients with an opportunity to explore issues and express feelings, conflicts, or problems using a variety of creative media such as music, writing, drawing, painting, or the use of clay. Group sessions can be unstructured and open ended, or they can be structured in a way that a specific theme or recovery issue (e.g., cravings, relapse, support systems, feelings, etc.) is explored. Such groups are often a safe way for clients to identify and express personal issues. Creative media helps clients tap unconscious material. Finished products as well as client participation in the group process often provides counselors with a wealth of information about the client.

In inpatient and partial hospital settings, these groups can be held several times each week for an hour or longer. In outpatient settings they can be held weekly, also for an hour and a half or longer.

Milieu Groups

These groups are usually used in inpatient or residential settings. They can be led by staff or clients. We have used the following milieu groups in our inpatient programs.

A *Morning Community Focus Group* is a client-led group that reviews the rules of the treatment program, the treatment activities for the day, assigns tasks to members of the community, and provides each member with the opportunity to state a goal they wish to work on during the day. Clients can complete a written daily goal planning worksheet to help guide them through this process. This group can be held up to seven days a week in inpatient settings.

An *Evening Community Focus Group* is a client-led group that reviews the day. Each client comments on his/her work during the day in relation to the goal that was set at the beginning of the day. Community concerns are also discussed in this meeting. Additionally clients have the opportunity to share positive feedback, words of encouragement, or thanks to others for positive things they have done during the day. This group can be held seven days a week in inpatient settings.

A *Community Group* is a staff and/or client-led group in which all clients and staff attend to discuss issues pertinent to the treatment community. If there are client-elected officers in the milieu, they can assume responsibility for running the meeting and ensuring that client concerns are brought up for discussion with staff present. This is also a mechanism in which staff can bring up issues that affect the milieu and reinforce program rules, policies, and philosophy. Regular community meetings often have a preventive effect, keeping little issues from becoming large ones that can have a severe, adverse impact on the overall client community. Special community meetings can be held when there are serious problems in the unit that are disruptive to the overall community.

This group is held up to five times per week in inpatient settings.

Relapse Prevention or Skill Groups

There are a variety of different relapse prevention or skill groups that can be used in dual diagnosis programs, throughout the continuum of care. Following is a brief description of various groups we have used. Many of these overlap with the **Psychoeducation** groups discussed in the next section.

Coping with Feelings groups teach cognitive and behavioral strategies to help clients cope more effectively with feelings. Specific areas focused on include anxiety and worry, guilt and shame, depression, boredom, and anger. Two sessions can be offered on each of these areas of feelings in order to ensure sufficient time is spent on strategies to cope with these various feelings. Although clients are commonly interested in every one of these feelings, they show the greatest interest in the coping with depression and coping with anger sessions as these are more problematic for the greater number of clients. Written materials such as recovery workbooks are used to supplement these group treatment sessions.

Relapse Prevention groups teach clients to anticipate and cope with the possibility of psychiatric or chemical dependency relapse. Group sessions can be provided on any of the following topics: understanding and coping with relapse warning signs; understanding and coping with high-risk relapse factors; craving and impulse control; coping with negative thinking; refusing alcohol and drug-use offers; developing a recovery network; leisure planning; and developing an aftercare plan. Coping with alcohol or drug lapse or relapse, or psychiatric relapse, is also discussed. Workbook assignments are used in these groups to help clients relate the material to their situations and to begin developing relapse prevention plans.

Cognitive Therapy groups teach clients methods to cope with cognitive distortions and negative thinking that commonly contribute to depression, anxiety, substance abuse, or other problems in life. Specific problems in thinking presented by clients are used to teach the cognitive concepts. This group can be held two-to-four times per week in inpatient settings and once a week in outpatient settings.

Problem Solving groups teach clients a step-by-step problem-solving process that can be applied to different life problems. Specific problems presented by clients are used to teach the problem-solving method. This group can be held twice per week in inpatient settings and once per week in outpatient settings.

Stress Management groups teach clients various ways of managing stress without needing to resort to using alcohol or other drugs. This group can be held weekly.

Psychoeducational Groups

Psychoeducational (PE) group sessions can easily be adapted to inpatient, residential, partial hospital, or outpatient settings. A specific PE group treatment curriculum can be developed for use in any treatment setting. (See next chapter for specific PE group curriculum.) PE group programs can vary in terms of number of sessions offered per week and total number of sessions offered during the treatment course. For example, clients in our various inpatient dual disorders programs participate in up to five PE groups per week. Outpatients attend weekly PE groups for three months.

PE groups aim to provide information on important recovery topics to clients and help them begin to explore different coping strategies to handle the various demands of recovery. It is important to try to balance the focus on *problems* and *coping strategies* so clients can begin to be exposed to positive strategies that can help them deal with their issues and problems. Each PE session has a recovery topic with objectives and key points to cover. Recovery workbook assignments are frequently used so that clients relate to the topic in a personal way.

Self-Help Groups

Clients should be provided information on various types of self-help groups for addiction (AA, NA, CA, Women for Sobriety, Rational Recovery), dual diagnosis (Double Trouble, Dual Recovery Anonymous, SAMI, CAMI, MISA, etc.), and mental health disorders (Emotions Anonymous, Recovery, and support groups for specific types of illness such as anxiety, mood, or schizophrenic disorders). Clients should also be exposed to support group meetings within the treatment setting, if available, and in the community. If possible, visits to local "recovery clubs" are highly recommended so that clients are exposed to this potentially excellent source of support.

Family Groups

A **Multiple Family Group (MFG)** aims to provide several families information about dual disorders and recovery, provide an opportunity to discuss their common concerns and problems, and offer support to each other. This group can be offered in all treatment settings on a weekly or monthly basis. MFG can be structured around a specific theme or topic related to dual disorders and recovery but should also offer a chance for participants to discuss things that are important to them. MFG sessions should be held at a time convenient to families and can last up to two hours. They usually include clients although some MFG sessions have been held solely for family members.

Another type of MFG is a **Family Psychoeducational Workshop (FPW)**. This is similar to an MFG in terms of the aims. The main difference is that a FPW can last much longer, up to an entire day. This provides staff with an opportunity to cover a wide range of topics while allowing plenty of time for the sharing of family issues and support among the various families. Workshops can be offered monthly or on a variable basis, depending on the needs of the families of a particular treatment system.

Recreational Groups

Recreational groups are an excellent way for clients to learn to have fun without alcohol or drugs. They help clients keep busy and participate in enjoyable activities. Some clients get to try new recreational activities, ones they weren't likely to have tried on their own. In addition, these groups offer a chance for clients to socialize and practice social skills. This is especially helpful for shy, isolated, or withdrawn clients who typically keep to themselves. Although counselors can offer specific types of recreational activities for clients to engage in, getting them to plan and carry out activities themselves usually has a greater therapeutic effect.

Team Communication

Group leaders and individual counselors should communicate regularly to share information regarding clients. This can be done during team meetings, by telephone, informally at the program site as staff encounter each other, or through brief written notes. For example, one of our clinicians, who conducts groups that other clinicians' clients are eligible to attend, uses a brief checklist that states the client's name, whether or not the client attended, cancelled or failed to show for the group, and any clinically significant information (e.g., client expresses an increase in suicidal ideation or reports a drug/alcohol relapse).

Developing a Dual Diagnosis Group Program

A dual diagnosis group program involving a variety of the aforementioned groups or other groups is an excellent way of provding comprehensive services to clients and families. A group program should be based on the diagnoses, problems, and level of functioning of clients, staff interest and availability, and length of stay of clients in treatment.

Staff from all disciplines should be involved in developing and conducting group programming. Even if a few select staff are designated as the *primary* group leaders, others can still be involved. For example, a psychiatrist can provide a group on causes and treatments of psychiatric illness; a physician's assistant or nurse can provide a group on medical aspects of alcohol and other drugs; or a social worker can provide a group on the impact of dual disorders on the family. Ancillary staff can also make a major contribution to a group program. For example, a pharmacist can provide a group on medication education or a group on the effects of alcohol and drugs on psychiatric medications. Or a priest, minister, or rabbi can provide a group on spirituality issues in recovery.

Some staff will be resistent to conducting group treatments because they feel inadequate in doing so, lack training in dual disorders treatment or group treatment in particular, do not value group treatments, or feel they are too busy at other things and cannot take the time to conduct group sessions. Strategies for working through this resistance include getting staff to participate in the planning of the group program, offering them education and training, providing an experienced group co-leader, setting the expectation that conducting group treatments is part of the job description, and providing regular group supervision. Over time, many staff will be able to work through this resistance although some will not.

Clients will sometimes be resistent to group treatments as well. In most cases, this resistance can be dealt with by providing an orientation about group treatments, discussing how groups can help a client's recovery, and discussing concerns and fears of a client regarding group participation. Occasionally, a new client to treatment may evidence extreme anxiety and fear of talking in groups and may have to be held out of groups until this anxiety and fear is under control. Or in inpatient settings clients who are decompensated in a psychotic or manic state will need time to stabilize before attending group sessions.

Some groups can also be based in level of functioning or time that clients have been alcohol or drug free. For example, in one of our inpatient dual diagnosis programs, lower functioning clients attend a separate dual recovery group than higher functioning clients. In our partial program, an advanced recovery group is offered to clients with several months of clean time. This provides them with an opportunity to focus on a variety of issues that would be difficult to address in a group whose members have been unable to establish much clean time. In our outpatient program, we offer stabilization and clean start groups to clients entering treatment. These focus on practical issues pertinent to stabilizing from psychiatric symptoms and achieving abstinence from alcohol or other drugs.

The group program can be modified over time as staff learn what works and what doesn't work with their client population. Eliciting client and family input is helpful in assessing their satisfaction with current group programming.

An orientation manual describing the various group treatments is a helpful way of providing information to clients regarding groups. This can also decrease some of their fears about groups.

It is important for clients to have access to individual treatment in addition to groups. Clients feel cheated if individual sessions aren't regularly provided. Although many do well in groups, they often have problems or issues that are easier to self-disclose in an individual session.

CHAPTER ELEVEN
Dual Recovery Psychoeducational Group Topics

Psychoeducational (PE) group sessions are structured around a specific recovery isue or theme. The specific themes reviewed depend on the total number of sessions available for the client. Each PE group is structured in the following way:

1. Topic or recovery theme
2. Objectives or purpose of PE group session
3. Major points to review and methods of covering the material
4. PE group handouts that are read aloud, completed, and discussed in group, allowing members to relate personally to the PE topic; or given to clients to review in-depth following the group session

The group leader reviews the material in an interactive way so that clients can ask questions, share personal experiences related to the material covered, and provide help and support to each other. Outpatient and partial hospital PE groups usually last one and one-half hours; inpatient PE group sessions usually last one hour.

Before reviewing the PE group topic material in outpatient groups, the leader first takes time to discuss whether any clients have had setbacks, lapses or relapses, close calls, strong cravings to use substances, or any other pressing issue since the last session. Some time is spent discussing these before reviewing the group curriculum. However, because this is not a therapy group, the leader should make sure that ample time is left for covering the PE group curriculum.

Following are examples of topics or recovery themes that can be explored in PE group sessions. Each of these sessions has a specific curriculum that follows this section of the manual. Most of these topics have specific sections in the client guide written by one of the authors (Daley) entitled *Dual Diagnosis Workbook: Recovery Strategies for Addiction and Mental Health Disorders,* (Independence, Missouri: Herald House/Independence Press; phone: 1-800-767-8181 or 816/252-5010). Group topics can be covered in more than one session if needed. For example, anger, depression, and relapse are issues often requiring several sessions. If the group leader has only a small number of sessions available, he/she should choose the topics most relevant to the client population.

1. Dual Disorders: Introduction and Overview
2. Psychiatric Illness
3. Understanding Addiction
4. Effects of Dual Disorders
5. Medical Effects of Alcohol and Drugs
6. Withdrawal from Alcohol and Other Drugs
7. Alcohol and Other Depressants

Some of these topics can also be modified and adapted for use in weekly multiple family groups of one and one-half hours duration, monthly one-half day, or day-long PE workshops attended by clients and families or significant others.

Any of the above themes as well as others may be explored in individual DDRC sessions. Counselors can use any of the aforementioned topics, or they can develop and add new group ideas as needed, based on the needs and concerns of their clients.

Psychoeducational groups can integrate reading and workbook assignments, and educational videos when possible. Using a multimedia approach helps to educate clients and begin teaching coping skills that are necessary for sober living.

An *interactive approach* is recommended so that clients are actively engaged in discussions of recovery issues and coping strategies. Some interactive methods include:

- Asking clients to identify coping strategies for particular issues or problems.
- Getting clients to participate in behavioral role-plays (e.g., to resist social pressure to use drugs or to express positive feelings).
- Getting clients to identify cognitive distortions and practice challenging these (e.g., making mountains out of molehills).
- Asking clients to share specific answers to workbook assignments.

An interactive approach is more likely to keep clients interested in the discussion, and it requires them to take responsibility to relate to material presented and discussed.

At the end of each group session are recommendations for recovery workbook and reading assignments, and educational videos that can be used to teach the content of the specific group topic.

PE GROUP #1
Dual Disorders:
Introduction and Overview

Objectives

- Define the terms "dual diagnosis" and "dual disorders" as a combination of chemical dependency and psychiatric illness.

- Identify symptoms of chemical dependency.

- Identify symptoms of psychiatric disorders.

- Identify multiple factors that contribute to the development and maintenance of chemical dependency or psychiatric illness.

- Identify possible relationships between chemical dependency and psychiatric illness.

Methods/Major Points

- Use lecture/discussion format. Write the major points on a chalkboard or flip chart in order to provide reinforcement.

- Review the following primary symptoms of addiction:

  1. Inappropriate, excessive, or compulsive use of alcohol or other drugs (also called compulsion)

  2. Preoccupation with getting or using chemicals (also called obsession)

  3. Tolerance changes (need for more to get the desired effect or getting high or drunk much easier, with less alcohol or drugs, than in the past)

  4. Difficulty cutting down or stopping alcohol or drugs once use begins (also called loss of control)

  5. Withdrawal symptoms (getting sick with symptoms specific to the types of chemicals used once they are stopped completely or reduced)

  6. Using alcohol or other drugs in order to avoid or stop withdrawal symptoms

  7. Continuing to use alcohol or other drugs even though they cause problems (medical, psychological, family, social, work, financial, etc.)

  8. Stopping alcohol or other drug use for a period of time only to return to using again

  9. Giving up important activities or relationships because of substance use

- Discuss categories of psychiatric disorders: Each has a cluster of specific symptoms relating to thinking, mood, behavior, or ability to function. Ask group to identify symptoms of psychiatric illness they are experiencing.

  1. Mood disorders
  2. Anxiety disorders
  3. Thought disorders
  4. Personality disorders
  5. Other addictive disorders

- Ask clients to state how their psychiatric problems affected their alcohol/drug use, and how their alcohol/drug use affected their psychiatric symptoms. Use this information to discuss the possible relationships between the various disorders.

  1. Each illness raises the risk of developing the other.
  2. Each illness affects recovery from the other.
  3. Chronic alcohol or drug use can cause or worsen psychiatric symptoms, mask them, or cause a psychiatric relapse.
  4. Each illness can become closely linked with the other over time.
  5. Each illness can develop at separate points in time.

- *Optional:* Have group members discuss previous treatment experiences in which only one of their disorders was addressed. Use this to emphasize the importance of addressing both disorders in recovery.

Supporting Materials

- Dennis C. Daley, *Dual Diagnosis Workbook: Recovery Strategies for Addiction and Mental Health Problems.* Session 2, "Understanding Mental Health and Addictive Disorders," pp. 10–17; Session 3, "Why I Came to Treatment," pp. 20–23. Independence, Missouri: Herald House/Independence Press, 1994.

PE GROUP #2
Psychiatric Illness

Objectives

- Define and identify types of psychiatric illness.
- Review major symptoms associated with various types of illness.
- Identify factors contributing to psychiatric illness.

Methods/Major Points

- Use lecture/discussion format. Write major points on a chalkboard or flip chart for reinforcement.

- Ask clients to define psychiatric illness. Then discuss psychiatric illness as a mental disorder or mental disease that involves biopsychosocial factors. Stress that psychiatric disorders are best viewed as "no-fault illnesses" and not a sign of "weakness."

- State that about 22.5 percent of adults in the United States will experience an episode of psychiatric illness at some point in their lives. The most common psychiatric disorders are mood disorders and anxiety disorders.

- Explain that a significant number of people with psychiatric disorders also have a substance use disorder.

- Define several different types of psychiatric illness.

    1. *Single episode*: Some people suffer only one episode of illness and once the symptoms remit, do not experience any more psychiatric problems.

    2. *Recurrent episodes*: Some people experience three or more discrete episodes over time. They may function well between episodes. Episodes of illness may be experienced years apart.

    3. *Chronic or persistent*: Some clients experience some psychiatric symptoms more or less all of the time. Even though they can get well and improve functioning, they may always have to cope with some of their symptoms.

- Ask clients to share some of the specific disorders or symptoms they are experiencing or have experienced in the past. Then discuss the general categories of psychiatric illness and types of symptoms associated with illness. Stress that each illness usually has a cluster of symptoms that together comprise a psychiatric diagnosis:

    1. Categories of illness among adults:

        a. Mood disorders

        b. Anxiety disorders

        c. Thought disorders

        d. Personality disorders

69

> e. Substance use disorders
>
> f. Eating disorders
>
> g. Other addictive disorders
>
> h. Organic disorders
>
> i. Adjustment disorders

2. Symptoms associated with various disorders:

> a. Emotional symptoms
>
> b. Cognitive symptoms
>
> c. Behavioral symptoms
>
> d. Personality symptoms

Supporting Materials

- Dennis C. Daley, *Dual Diagnosis Workbook: Recovery Strategies for Addiction and Mental Health Problems*. Session 2, "Understanding Mental Health and Addictive Disorders," pp. 12–17.

PE GROUP #3
Understanding Addiction

Objectives

• Define addiction as a "no-fault" disease with specific symptoms.

• Identify symptoms of addiction.

• Identify biopsychosocial factors contributing to the development and maintennce of addiction.

Methods/Major Points

• Use lecture/discussion format. Write major points on a chalkboard or flip chart for reinforcement.

• Explain that more than 16 percent of adults in the United States will experience a substance use disorder at some point in their lives. A significant number of people with a substance use disorder also will experience a psychiatric disorder at some point in their lives.

• Ask clients to state their definitions of addiction. Then state that the American Medical Association has classified addiction as a disease. A disease is a "syndrome" with a "cluster of specific symptoms." Similar to many medical and psychiatric disorders, addiction has a set of symptoms.

• Ask clients to share examples of specific symptoms of addiction that they have experienced. State that contrary to what many people believe, most of the symptoms are behavioral, not physical. Even in the absence of physical symptoms, a severe problem with alcohol and drugs can exist.

• Ask group to identify the symptoms and signs of chemical dependency that they have experienced. Provide additional examples of major symptoms that group members fail to mention. Symptoms to review include:

1. Excessive or inappropriate use of chemicals (alcohol or other drugs): getting high or drunk and not being able to fulfill obligations at home, work, or with others; feeling like chemicals are needed in order to fit in with others or function at work or home; driving under the influence.

2. Preoccupation with getting or using chemicals: living mainly to get high on alcohol or drugs; chemical use becomes too important in life; being obsessed with using.

3. Tolerance changes: needing more of the chemical to get high; or getting high much easier or with less of the chemical than in the past.

71

4. Having trouble cutting down or stopping once you drink or take drugs: not being able to control how much or how often chemicals are used; using more alcohol or drugs than planned.

5. Withdrawal symptoms: getting sick physically once the person cuts down or stops using (for example, having the shakes, feeling nauseous, having gooseflesh, having a runny nose, etc.); or experiencing mental symptoms such as depression, anxiety, or agitation.

6. Using to avoid or stop withdrawal symptoms: using chemicals constantly to prevent withdrawal sickness; drinking or using drugs in order to stop withdrawal symptoms.

7. Using alcohol or other drugs even though they cause problems in life: not taking the advice of a doctor, therapist, or some other professional to stop using because of problems chemicals have caused in life.

8. Giving up important activities or losing friendships because of substance use: stopping activities that once were important; giving up friends who don't get high; losing friends because of alcohol and drug use and how it affects relationships with others.

9. Stopping use for a period of time (days, weeks, or months), only to go back again: making temporary promises to quit only to go back to getting high again; being unable to sustain abstinence.

10. Getting into trouble because of alcohol or drug use: losing jobs or being unable to find a job; getting arrested or having other legal problems; losing relationships or having trouble with family or friends; or having money problems.

11. Blackouts: forgetting what one did or said while under the influence of chemicals.

- Ask clients to state the factors they think contributed to developing an addiction. Inquire as to whether they have any family members with an addiction (currently or in the past).

- Review addiction as a progressive, potentially fatal, biopsychosocial disease. Factors contributing to addiction include:

1. Physical:
    - first-degree relatives of addicted people have increased odds of becoming addicted;
    - addicted people may be born with or develop deficiencies in certain chemicals in the brain;
    - they may more easily develop a tolerance to the effects of alcohol or other drugs;
    - some alcoholics are less able to read body cues that too much alcohol has been ingested.

2. Psychological or emotional:
    - people with psychiatric illness are more vulnerable to developing an addiction compared to the general population;
    - certain personality traits or styles may increase a person's vulnerability to addiction;
    - people who rely on alcohol or other drugs to deal with stress or uncomfortable emotions may gradually develop a dependency over time.

72

3. Social or cultural:
   - availability of alcohol or drugs;
   - influence of peers and social groups;
   - community norms governing substance use behavior.

- State that once an addiction develops, it takes on a life of its own. At this point, no reason is needed for using chemicals as the addiction itself causes one to use.

- State that addiction is very treatable. Most people who participate in treatment or self-help groups improve. For individuals with coexisting psychiatric illness, abstinence from alcohol or other drugs is necessary to experience the full benefits of recovery.

Supporting Materials

- Dennis C. Daley, *Dual Diagnosis Workbook: Recovery Strategies for Addiction and Mental Health Problems*. Session 2, "Understanding Mental Health and Addictive Disorders," pp. 10–11, 15–17. Independence, Missouri: Herald House/Independence Press, 1994.

- Dennis C. Daley, *Surviving Addiction Workbook*. Session 1, pp. 1–2. Holmes Beach, Florida: Learning Publications, 1-800-222-1525.

- Merlene Miller, Terence T. Gorski, and David K. Miller, *Learning to Live Again: A Guide for Recovery from Chemical Dependency,* Updated and Revised Edition. Chapters 1–3, pp. 11–36. Independence, Missouri: Herald House/Independence Press, 1992.

PE GROUP #4
Effects of Dual Disorders

Objectives

- Clients learn that either or both disorders can affect any area of functioning: medical, psychiatric, emotional, family, social, interpersonal, occupational, academic, legal, spiritual, and financial.
- Identify various adverse effects of alcohol and drug use on group members' psychiatric condition and other aspects of their life.
- Identify effects of their psychiatric illness on substance use and other areas of life.
- Introduce the concept of "progression of illness" and that left untreated, either or both disorders can lead to a worsening of symptoms or functioning over time.

Methods/Major Points

- Use a lecture/discussion format. Write the major points discussed on a chalkboard or flip chart for reinforcement.
- Ask clients how they think their alcohol or other drug use has affected their psychiatric symptoms and other areas of their life.
- Ask clients how they think their psychiatric condition has affected their use of alcohol/drugs or other problems in their life.
- Review common problems associated with either or both disorders provided by group members. Add additional examples if needed of problems caused or worsened by either or both illnesses:

  1. Physical health or medical
  2. Diet and eating habits
  3. Sexual desire or behavior
  4. Exercise habits
  5. Self-esteem or confidence
  6. Relationships with family
  7. Relationships with friends or coworkers
  8. Spirituality

74

9. Work or school

10. Lost opportunities or wasted talents or abilities

11. Hobbies or leisure interests

12. Financial condition

13. Difficulty with the law or other legal problems

- Discuss how continued involvement in treatment provides an opportunity to cope with problems caused or worsened by dual disorders as well as reduce the odds of further harm. State that either illness can worsen without treatment, a condition referred to as "progression."

Supporting Materials

- Dennis C. Daley. *Dual Diagnosis Workbook: Recovery Strategies for Addiction and Mental Health Problems*—Session 5, "Effects of Dual Disorders on My Life," pp. 27–29; session 9, "Medical and Psychiatric Effects of Drugs and Alcohol," pp. 38–40.

- Dennis C. Daley. *Surviving Addiction Workbook.* Section 4, "Evaluating the Effects of Your Addiction," pp. 7–8. Holmes Beach, Florida: Learning Publications (1-800-222-1525).

- Videotape: *Double Trouble: Coping with Chemical Dependency and Mental Health Disorders—Parts I and II.* Gerald T. Rogers Productions (1-800-227-9100).

PE GROUP #5
Medical Effects of Alcohol and Drugs

Objectives

- Identify factors that mediate the effects of alcohol or other drugs on the body.
- Identify common physical and medical problems associated with substance use and addiction.
- Clients learn to identify specific medical effects of their alcohol and other drug use.
- Clients are introduced to good physical and health-care habits that can facilitate their ongoing recovery.

Methods

- Use lecture/discussion format. Write major points on a chalkboard or flip chart for reinforcement.
- State that substance use and addiction are associated with many different medical problems and diseases. The specific effects on a given individual will depend on the following factors:

    1. Type, frequency, and quantity of substance use over time.
    2. Methods of drug ingesting (e.g., using needles, smoking, etc.).
    3. Impurities in drugs or dirty needles, cotton, or rinsing water (for IV drug abusers).
    4. How chemicals affect judgment and behavior. For example, poor judgment can lead to accidents while under the influence of chemicals or involvement in high-risk behaviors such as unprotected sex, fights, or criminal acts.
    5. Diet.
    6. Overall health and lifestyle.

- Ask clients to identify specific physical and medical effects of their use of alcohol or other drugs.
- Build on the examples provided by clients. Review common examples of physical and medical effects of substance use:

    1. Accidents and injuries, including serious ones and close-to-death experiences
    2. Central nervous system problems (blackouts, memory problems, convulsions, slower reflexes, etc.)
    3. Serious complications related to an overdose or severe withdrawal syndromes
    4. Digestive system problems (cancers of the mouth, tongue, pharynx, and esophagus; ulcers, gastritis, pancreatitis, etc.)

76

5. Liver disease

6. HIV+ or AIDS

7. Cardiovascular system problems (weakening of heart muscle, irregular heartbeat, heart pain, heart attack, stroke, and high blood pressure)

8. Respiratory system problems (lung disease and damage, infections, etc.)

9. Sexual problems (diseases, problems with performance, problems with menstrual cycle, etc.)

10. Worsening of existing medical conditions such as hypertension, diabetes, etc.

11. Loss of teeth or poor dental hygiene

12. Poor overall health including significant loss or gain of weight unintentionally

- State that as a result of these and other medical complications, people with addictions use medical services more frequently than others. The life span can be shortened due to the chronic effects of chemical use over time. Hundreds of thousands of people die every year from the direct and indirect effects of alcohol and drugs.

- Emphasize the importance of the following physical and medical health issues in recovery:

  1. getting a good physical workup and medical help for existing problems;

  2. getting a good dental workup and help for existing problems;

  3. adhering to a healthy diet and avoiding getting too hungry (remember HALT);

  4. getting sufficient rest and sleep;

  5. exercising; and

  6. participating in stress reduction and stress management activities (e.g., relaxation, meditation, etc.).

Supporting Materials

- Dennis C. Daley, *Dual Diagnosis Workbook: Recovery Strategies for Addiction and Mental Health Problems*—Session 9 "Medical and Psychiatric Effects of Drugs and Alcohol," pp. 38–40.

- Dennis C. Daley, *Surviving Addiction Workbook*—Section 6, "Physical Recovery," pp. 10–11. Holmes Beach, Florida: Learning Publications, 1-800-222-1525.

- Merlene Miller, Terence T. Gorski, and David K. Miller, *Learning to Live Again: A Guide for Recovery from Chemical Dependency*, Updated and Revised Edition. pp. 37–50. Independence, Missouri: Herald House/Independence Press, 1-800-767-8181.

Withdrawal from Alcohol and Other Drugs: Physical and Emotional Symptoms

Objectives

- Identify physical and emotional symptoms of withdrawal from alcohol or other drugs.

- Define the following terms: acute withdrawal syndrome and protracted withdrawal syndrome (also referred to as post acute withdrawal).

- Identify methods commonly used to manage withdrawal symptoms associated with addiction.

Methods/Major Points

- Use lecture/discussion format. Write major points on a chalkboard or flip chart for reinforcement.

- State that both physical and emotional symptoms are associated with withdrawal from addictive use of chemicals. The intensity and duration of these symptoms depend on the severity of the addiction (types, amounts, frequency of substance use, and methods of ingestion) and clients' overall health.

- Ask clients to give personal examples of physical and emotional withdrawal symptoms that they experienced when first coming off of alcohol or other drugs. Define the early withdrawal period as "acute withdrawal." State that this usually only lasts a few days or longer, depending on the specific chemicals a client has been using.

- Ask clients to give personal examples of symptoms experienced weeks or months into recovery. State that some people experience a "protracted withdrawal" (post acute withdrawal) long after they stop using chemicals. The body may take months or longer to adjust to abstinence.

- State that specific types of withdrawal symptoms relate to the types of chemicals clients have been using. Emphasize that withdrawal from alcohol or barbiturate dependence is potentially the most dangerous due to the possibility of seizures. If needed, give examples of withdrawal symptoms from the following categories of chemicals:

  1. Alcohol and other depressants

  2. Opiates or narcotics

  3. Cocaine and other stimulants

- Review the following list of examples of physical and emotional symptoms associated with withdrawal from various chemicals:

    1. Shakes or tremors

    2. Anxiety or agitation

    3. Intense cravings for alcohol or other drugs

    4. Sleep problems

    5. Depression

    6. Runny nose, tearing eyes, gooseflesh

    7. Severe cramps, nausea, or feeling worn out

    8. Confusion or difficulty thinking clearly

    9. Convulsions or seizures

- Ask clients how they have treated their withdrawal symptoms in the past (most will probably report continued ingestion of alcohol or other drugs as the main way they prevented or attenuated their withdrawal symptoms).

- Review medical and psychological strategies used to treat withdrawal syndromes:

    1. Medications

    2. Rest and proper diet

    3. Supportive care for professionals

- Review other strategies to cope with withdrawal symptoms:

    1. Getting support from others (family, sponsor, etc.);

    2. Gaining education about withdrawal symptoms and talking about one's symptoms;

    3. Avoiding high-risk social situations in which alcohol or other drugs will be present;

    4. Getting rid of alcohol or drugs to reduce the chance of using to stop withdrawal symptoms; and

    5. Remembering that withdrawal is a temporary phenomenon.

Supporting Materials

- Merlene Miller, Terence T. Gorski, and David K. Miller, *Learning to Live Again: A Guide for Recovery from Chemical Dependency,* Updated and Revised Edition, pp. 103–128. Independence, Missouri: Herald House/Independence Press, 1992.

Alcohol and Other Depressants

Objectives

- Review the pharmacology of alcohol and other depressants.

- Identify medical problems associated with alcohol and other depressant abuse and dependence.

- Identify psychosocial and psychiatric problems associated with alcohol and other depressant abuse and dependence.

Methods/Major Points

- Use a lecture/discussion format. Write the major points discussed on a chalkboard or flip chart for reinforcement.

- State that there are many different types of Central Nervous System (CNS) depressant drugs. These include the following:

  1. Alcohol

  2. Hypnotics, such as barbiturates and barbiturate-like drugs

  3. Antianxiety drugs (also called minor tranquilizers), such as the benzodiazepines

- CNS depressant drugs are used to treat medical and/or psychiatric problems. Some are much more addictive than others.

- These drugs have a variety of physical, behavioral, and psychological effects, depending on types and amounts used and the psychological state of the user. CNS depressant drugs are dangerous when taken in large doses and can cause death by coma or convulsions. The CNS depressant drug withdrawal syndrome is more severe than any other type of drug withdrawal.

- Symptoms associated with excessive use of CNS depressant drugs or withdrawal include anxiety, depression, sleep disturbance, impaired judgment, impaired coordination, slurred speech, tremors, weakness, nausea and vomiting, memory loss or blackouts, seizures, and confusion.

- State that hundreds of thousands of people die each year from the direct and indirect effects of alcohol. Due to the acute and chronic effects of alcohol or other depressant use, poor diet or health care practices, or concurrent use of tobacco the risk of medical and psychiatric problems is higher among alcoholics compared to the general population. Ask clients to provide examples of medical problems caused or worsened by their drinking or use of other depressant drugs. Then, state that alcoholism is associated with the following medical disorders:

80

1. Ulcer disease
2. Gastritis (inflammation of the stomach)
3. Pancreatitis (inflammation of the pancreas)
4. Liver disease
5. Cancers of the esophagus, stomach, head and neck, and lungs.
6. Organic brain diseases
7. Peripheral neuropathy (deterioration of peripheral nerves to hands or feet)
8. Heart disease
9. Sexual disorders
10. Trauma caused by accidents or head injury

- Ask clients to provide examples of psychosocial problems caused or worsened by their alcoholism or drug addiction. Then, review the following problems associated with alcoholism or other forms of addiction to CNS depressant drugs:

   1. Accidents
   2. Violence
   3. Driving impairment
   4. Anxiety and panic symptoms
   5. Depression
   6. Antisocial behaviors
   7. Suicidal feelings or actual attempts
   8. Work, family, legal, financial, and other psychosocial problems

- Other points that can be stressed during this session include:

   1. Alcohol in beer has the same effect as alcohol in other beverages.
   2. The legal limit for intoxication is a blood alcohol level (BAL) of .10 in most states. The higher the BAL, the greater the likelihood that the client will get in an accident.
   3. If a client does not "feel drunk" after consuming a large quantity of alcohol it is probably due to a high tolerance. However, even if a client doesn't feel drunk, judgment, behavior, and ability will definitely be impaired. Some clients with a high BAL feel "normal" and believe that they can drive safely or function adequately.
   4. Mixing alcohol with other depressant drugs potentiates their effects. It's kind of like having this formula: 2+2=6.
   5. Alcohol use, even in small quantities, can lead to very poor judgment, causing a person to say or do things that would not occur if not under the influence of alcohol.

6. Some people believe that alcohol gives a person "courage" to say what is really on the mind. In reality, the "truth" that comes out can be greatly distorted or exaggerated. For example, mild irritation may be expressed as passionate hatred, or attraction may falsely be stated as deep love.

7. Victims and perpetrators of homicide and other forms of violence often are under the influence of alcohol during the violent episode.

Supporting Materials

*   Many publishers, including AA World Services and the National Clearinghouse for Alcohol and Drug Information (NCADI: 1-800-729-6686) have informational guides on alcohol and other drugs.

PE GROUP #8
Cocaine and Other Stimulants

Objectives

- Review the pharmacology of cocaine and other stimulant drugs.
- Identify medical problems associated with cocaine and other stimulants.
- Identify psychosocial and psychiatric problems associated with cocaine and other stimulants.

Methods/Major Points

- Use a lecture/discussion format. Write the major points discussed on a chalkboard or flip chart for reinforcement.
- State that there are several types of stimulant drugs, including the following:

  1. Cocaine and crack/cocaine
  2. Amphetamines
  3. Caffeine
  4. Nicotine

- Stimulant drugs are widely prescribed in the treatment of narcolepsy, attention deficit disorder with hyperactivity, obesity, and depression. Excessive use of them can cause symptoms that mimic a variety of psychiatric symptoms.
- These drugs can be taken in the form of pills, injected with a needle, or smoked in the form of freebase cocaine or crack/cocaine. Sometimes stimulants such as cocaine are mixed with heroin and injected. Many people use alcohol to help them cope with the "crash" associated with coming off of a cocaine or speed binge.
- More recently there has been a significant increase in the abuse of crack/cocaine, a cheap form of smokable cocaine that can be bought in the form of "rocks" for as little as $3–5.
- Stimulant drugs release neurotransmitters such as norepinephrine (NE) from nerve cells. These also cause a decrease in the reuptake of the neurotransmitter dopamine (DA).
- These drugs cause feelings of euphoria, increase energy, decrease fatigue, decrease the need for sleep, decrease appetite, and sometimes increase sexual feelings and sexual energy. Medical problems associated with cocaine and other stimulants include:

  1. an increase in the heart rate and an elevation of blood pressure which can cause hemorrhaging in the cranium;
  2. increase in heart rate, which can cause cardiac fibrillation, respiratory arrest, and death;

83

3. pulmonary problems such as bronchitis;

4. complications associated with using contaminated needles such as hepatitis, abscesses, AIDS virus, or endocarditis;

5. damage to the nasal septum (for snorters of cocaine); and

6. damage to a fetus in pregnant women.

- These drugs, especially crack/cocaine, cause a variety of serious psychiatric and psychosocial problems. Ask group members to give examples and add additional examples as needed to cover the following problems:

  1. Accidents
  2. Violence
  3. Psychosis, including paranoia
  4. Panic symptoms
  5. Depression, especially when coming off of a binge
  6. Antisocial behaviors
  7. Suicidal feelings and attempts
  8. Impulsive behaviors
  9. Work, family, legal, financial, and other problems

- Other points that can be stressed during this session include:

  1. Many people with stimulant addiction also have a serious problem with alcohol or other drugs.
  2. Abstinence from alcohol and all drugs is important for recovery to progress. Continuing to drink alcohol or smoke pot, for example, significantly raises the risk of relapse to cocaine use.

Supporting Materials

- Dennis C. Daley, *Living Sober: An Interactive Video Recovery Program—Client Workbook*. Section 9, "Recovering from Crack/Cocaine Addiction," 1994, pp. 24–26. Skokie, Illinois: Gerald T. Rogers Productions (1-800-227-9100).

- Roger D. Weiss and Steven M. Mirin, *Cocaine*. New York: Ballantine Books, 1987.

- Videotape: *Living Sober: Recovery from Crack/Cocaine Addiction,* 1994: Skokie, Illinois: Gerald T. Rogers Productions, 1-800-227-9100.

PE GROUP #9
Heroin and Other Opiates

Objectives

- Review the pharmacology of heroin and other opiates.
- Identify medical problems associated with heroin and other opiates.
- Identify psychosocial and psychiatric problems associated with opiate abuse and dependence.

Methods/Major Points

- Use a lecture/discussion format. Write the major points discussed on a chalkboard or flip chart for reinforcement.
- State that there are many different types of opiate drugs. These include street drugs and prescription drugs such as pain medications. Opiate drugs can be ingested by using a needle (IV), snorting, smoking, or taking in pill form. Some addicts mix stimulants such as cocaine with heroin.
- Opiate drugs include the following:

  1. Heroin
  2. Opium
  3. Methadone
  4. Prescription drugs such as Dilaudid, Percodan, Darvon, and Demerol

- Some opiate drugs used medically as painkillers.
- Opiate drugs have a variety of physical, behavioral, and psychological effects, depending on types and amounts used, methods of ingesting, and the psychological state of the user. Opiate drugs are dangerous when taken in large doses and can cause death by coma. The opiate withdrawal syndrome is not as severe or life threatening as drugs such as alcohol or barbiturates, although it has been presented as life threatening.
- Symptoms associated with excessive use of opiate drugs or withdrawal include runny nose, yawning, tearing eyes, sweating, tremor, sleep and appetite disturbance, weakness, chills, cramping and abdominal pain, gooseflesh, and strong drug cravings.
- Opiate addicts can die from the direct and indirect effects of opiates including overdoses, suicides, homicides, and medical problems such as AIDS which is frequently transmitted by sharing dirty cotton, rinsing water, or needles.
- Ask clients to provide examples of medical problems caused or worsened by their opiate drug use. Then, review medical problems associated with opiate addiction:

85

1. AIDS
2. Skin and muscle abscesses and infections
3. Liver disease
4. Tetanus or malaria
5. Gastric ulcers
6. Kidney failure
7. Endocarditis
8. Heart arrhythmias
9. Sexual dysfunctions

- Ask clients to provide examples of psychosocial or psychiatric problems caused or worsened by their opiate addiction. Then, review the following problems associated with opiate addiction:

  1. Accidental drug overdoses
  2. Depression
  3. Antisocial and criminal behaviors, including violence, which are committed to get money to buy the drugs
  4. Suicidal feelings or actual attempts
  5. Work, family, legal, financial, and other psychosocial problems

- Other points that can be stressed during this session include:

  1. Many opiate addicts abuse other drugs or transfer their addiction to other chemicals such as alcohol or cocaine once they stop using opiates.
  2. Drugs such as heroin are "cut" with a variety of adulterants that can be dangerous when ingested.
  3. Opiate addicts unable to get and stay drug free with rehabilitation programs, counseling, and/or NA may benefit from Methadone Maintenance (MM). However, while MM was designed to be used for two years or less, many adicts stay on MM for years and years. Drug addicts often report it is very difficult to get off of MM, especially after years of taking Methadone.

Supporting Materials

- Many publishers, including NA World Services and the National Clearinghouse for Alcohol and Drug Information (NCADI: 1-800-727-6686) have information guides on heroin and other forms of drug abuse.

PE GROUP #10
Psychosocial Effects of Alcohol and Drugs

Objectives

- Identify common psychosocial problems caused or worsened by substance abuse and addiction.

- Clients identify specific psychosocial problems experienced as a result of their substance use.

- Clients identify strategies to begin coping with these problems.

Methods/Major Points

- Use lecture/discussion format. Write major points on a chalkboard or flip chart for reinforcement.

- State that addiction is associated with a variety of psychological or emotional, psychiatric, family, interpersonal, social, academic, occupational, legal, spiritual, and financial problems. Addiction causes new problems or makes existing ones much worse.

- Substance use is also a way to avoid facing one's problems.

- Ask clients to give examples of specific problems caused or worsened by their addiction in one or more of the areas listed below. Use their examples and add new ones as needed in order to summarize some of the common problems associated with addiction. Try to cover some examples from each of the following categories:

    1. Psychological or emotional
    2. Psychiatric
    3. Family
    4. Interpersonal
    5. Social
    6. Academic
    7. Occupational
    8. Legal
    9. Spiritual
    10. Financial

- Discuss the importance of working on resolving some of these problems as recovery progresses. Emphasize the importance of limiting the number of problems addressed so that clients don't feel overwhelmed.
- Ask clients to choose one problem caused by their addiction that they would like to begin working on.
- Ask several clients to describe a problem and identify cognitive and behavioral coping strategies that can help them deal with this problem. Ask other clients for additional ideas on coping strategies.

Supporting Materials

- Dennis C. Daley, *Dual Diagnosis Workbook: Recovery Strategies for Addiction and Mental Health Problems*. Session 5, "Effects of Dual Disorders on My Life," pp. 27–29.
- Dennis C. Daley, *Surviving Addiction Workbook*, pp. 6–11, pp. 10–22. Holmes Beach, Florida: Learning Publications, 1-800-222-1525.
- Merlene Miller, Terence T. Gorski, and David K. Miller, *Learning to Live Again: A Guide for Recovery from Chemical Dependency*, Updated and Revised Edition. Chapter 5, "Psychological Effects," pp. 51–60; and chapter 6, "Social Effects," pp. 61–66. Independence, Missouri: Herald House/Independence Press.

How to Use Treatment:
Keys to Successful Recovery

Objectives

- Clients identify their expectations regarding treatment and recovery.
- Explain the importance of clients taking an "active" role in recovery and taking responsibility for change.
- Show the benefits and limitations of professional treatment.
- Identify attitudes and behaviors that promote a more positive recovery.

Methods

- Use lecture/discussion format. Write major points on a chalkboard or flip chart for reinforcement.
- State that it is important for clients to have realistic expectations regarding treatment and recovery. Unrealistic expectations, especially those that are too high, will set clients up to fail, feel frustrated, or feel disappointed.
- Ask clients to discuss their expectations regarding professional treatment. Some questions to discuss are:

  1. What do clients hope to get from treatment?

  2. How do clients see their role in the recovery process?

  3. How do clients view responsibility in terms of treatment compliance and trying out new behaviors?

- Stress the importance of clients taking an "active" role in treatment. This means they work closely with their treatment team to identify problems they need to work on, identify changes they want to make, and implement strategies to cope with these problems and make changes.

- Review the ways that treatment can help as well as some of the limitations of treatment and the professionals providing it. For example:

  1. A therapist will not always be available for telephone discussions and may not be able to give counseling appointments as often as clients would like.

  2. A therapist or other professional can't solve the client's problems.

  3. Even medications may have a limited impact on some psychiatric symptoms. It isn't always easy to find the right medication, and doctors have differing ideas on what types of medications to use.

4. Changing therapists or doctors is not always easy. The client needs time to adjust to any change in treatment team members, whether it happened because the therapist or doctor changed jobs or the client changed treatment providers.

- Ask clients to discuss attitudes and behaviors that will help their long-term recovery. Add additional points as needed and review the following positive attitudes and behaviors:

    1. being honest with treatment team, sponsor, and self about problems, struggles, feelings, and thoughts;

    2. being patient and persistent regarding change;

    3. making a commitment to recovery and change;

    4. complying with treatment (attending treatment sessions and making appointments on time);

    5. being self-reflective;

    6. being realistic regarding recovery and change;

    7. setting realistic goals for change;

    8. sharing goals with others and asking for additional feedback;

    9. knowing when to ask others for help and support;

    10. working hard at recovery by learning new coping strategies to deal with problems;

    11. attending support groups;

    12. allowing room for mistakes and learning from them;

    13. evaluating progress from time to time and changing the treatment plan as needed; and

    14. developing "inner resources" and learning ways to help oneself.

Supporting Materials

- Dennis C. Daly, *Living Sober: An Interactive Video Recovery Program—Client Workbook.* pp. 1–2. Gerald T. Rogers Productions (1-800-227-9100).

PE GROUP #12

Phases of Recovery from Dual Disorders

Objectives

- Clients are introduced to the concept of "phases of recovery" from dual disorders.
- Identify the key issues for each of the phases of recovery.

Methods/Major Points

- Use lecture/discussion format. Write major points on a chalkboard or flip chart for reinforcement.

- State that there are six possible phases of recovery for dual disorders. Each phase has some specific issues related to the psychiatric illness, addiction, or both. These phases are "rough" guidelines as not everyone progresses through them at the same pace or in the same way. The severity of the illnesses and the clients' motivation are key variables affecting how they progress through these phases.

- Review each of these six phases to summarize key themes. Ask clients to react to the material presented according to their experiences.

PHASE 1—Transition and Engagement:

1. Become engaged in treatment and recognize the need for ongoing involvement in treatment.
2. Recognize an inability to control the use of alcohol or other drugs and the effects of use on psychiatric symptoms (covering up, triggering off, or worsening psychiatric symptoms).
3. Recognize the existence of a psychiatric disorder that needs treatment and that an untreated disorder will interfere with recovery from addiction.
4. Entering treatment may result from an involuntary commitment or pressure from family or others to get help.
5. Recognize ambivalence about recovery.
6. Getting the family or significant others involved in treatment.
7. Lasts several weeks or longer.

91

PHASE 2—Stabilization:

1. Stabilize from acute psychiatric symptoms.
2. Get alcohol and drugs out of the system and adjust to being chemically free.
3. Become educated about the addictive and psychiatric illnesses, the role of professional therapy, the role of medications, and the role of self-help programs in ongoing recovery.
4. Learn about and accept diagnoses.
5. Develop trust in the treatment team.
6. Learn how to cope with thoughts of using or cravings for alcohol or drugs.
7. Learn to cope with symptoms and problems associated with the psychiatric illness.
8. Get involved in self-help programs.
9. Strengthen motivation to recover.
10. Accept the need for long-term involvement in professional treatment and self-help recovery.
11. Develop a problem list to work on during recovery.
12. Accept the need for total abstinence from alcohol, street drugs, and nonprescribed drugs as the path to take in recovery.
13. Continue family involvement in treatment.
14. Lasts several weeks or longer.

PHASE 3—Early Recovery:

1. Continue recovery work from Phase 2.
2. Avoid people, places, and things that represent a relapse risk for addiction.
3. Learn nonchemical ways of coping with pressures from others to use alcohol or other drugs, and coping with situations that in the past led to using chemicals.
4. Continue to challenge and change addictive thinking, and learn to change negative thinking contributing to psychiatric symptoms.
5. Continue to learn ways to cope with psychiatric symptoms, especially chronic and persistent ones.
6. Accept the reality that medications can help reduce symptoms but other personal and lifestyle changes are necessary for recovery to progress.
7. Change behaviors, especially ones that caused difficulties in the past.
8. Build structure and regularity into day-to-day life to keep busy, stay focused on recovery issues, get involved in enjoyable leisure activities, and limit the amount of free time.

9. Continue family work and learn about the impact of the dual disorders and behaviors on the family.

10. Continue involvement in support groups and working with a sponsor.

11. Address guilt and shame issues.

12. Lasts three to six months.

PHASE 4—Middle Recovery:

1. Continue work from Phase 3.

2. Increase self-disclosure about inner thoughts, feelings, and problems.

3. Make amends to family and other significant people hurt by behaviors.

4. Accept reality of lost relationships that cannot be repaired or salvaged.

5. Learn ways to improve communication and strengthen interpersonal relationships.

6. Focus on spirituality issues.

7. Continue improving cognitive and behavioral coping strategies to deal with negative or upsetting thoughts and feelings and problems.

8. Learn to identify and manage warning signs of relapse of psychiatric illness.

9. Learn to identify and manage warning signs of addiction relapse.

10. Monitor recovery on a daily basis.

11. Continue to take medications for recurrent or chronic forms of psychiatric illness.

12. Lasts six to twelve months.

PHASE 5 —Late Recovery:

1. Continue work from middle recovery phase.

2. Focus on changing character defects or personality traits.

3. Continue developing more positive values and meaning in life.

4. Increase awareness of "inner self" (defenses, personality traits, values, strengths, and vulnerabilities).

5. Gain greater understanding of past influences on current behaviors, values and relationships.

6. Deal with family-of-origin issues if needed in order to heal from past emotional pain.

7. Broaden support group involvement if needed to include ACOA or survivor groups.

8. Focus more on "lifestyle balancing" so that attention is directed to all major areas of life — recovery, work, love, relationships, fun, and spirituality.

9. Lasts a year or longer.

PHASE 6—Maintenance:

1. An ongoing phase in which the work of recovery continues with less reliance on a therapist or sponsor.

2. Increased attention is directed toward "giving away" what one learned in recovery by sponsoring others or serving the greater good of society.

3. No time limit as some people continue involvement in professional treatment, self-help programs, or a self-management program of change for an indefinite period of time.

• State that lapses or relapses to addiction, recurrences of psychiatric symptoms, or other life setbacks are dealt with as they occur throughout recovery. A setback or relapse does not necessarily mean that the client starts all over again.

Supporting Materials

• Dennis C. Daley, *Dual Diagnosis Workbook: Recovery Strategies for Addiction and Mental Health Problems.* Session 12, "Recovery from Dual Disorders," pp. 55–65.

• Terence T. Gorski, *Passages through Recovery: An Action Plan for Preventing Relapse,* pp. 3–9. Center City, Minnesota: Hazelden, 1989 (1-800-328-9000).

Developing a Problem List
For Dual Recovery

Objectives

- Clients learn the importance of developing a problem list for use in treatment sessions and in devising recovery goals.
- Clients incorporate addiction, psychiatric, and other important lifestyle problems on the master problem list.
- Clients learn that there are some fairly common problems associated with dual disorders (intrapersonal and interpersonal).
- Clients identify personal strengths.

Methods/Main Points

- Use lecture/discussion format. Write major points on a chalkboard or flip chart for reinforcement.
- Ask clients to state some of the specific problems that brought them to treatment. These may be specific psychiatric disorders, addictive disorders, symptoms or problems associated with either or both of the dual disorders, or other pertinent psychosocial problems.
- Emphasize that during the early stages of recovery, the main emphasis is on stabilizing acute psychiatric symptoms and getting alcohol and drug free. Ask clients why it is important to get sober or clean for recovery to progress.
- Discuss the importance of prioritizing problems and limiting the focus on a few in early recovery so that clients don't try to deal with too many problems too early in the recovery process.
- Discuss the importance of not just focusing on problems, but on identifying and building on personal strengths. Every client has some personal strengths, regardless of why he/she came to treatment. Ask clients to identify their own strengths. Give some examples if needed in order to help clients know that strengths are:

  1. Positive qualities such as being friendly, sociable, kind, committed, resourceful, or assertive.
  2. Talents such as athletic, music, artistic, mechanical, or other abilities.
  3. Faith in God or a belief in a Higher Power.
  4. Positive relationships with family, friends, AA/NA members, professional caregivers, or others.
  5. Positive attitudes about recovery and willingness to work hard.
  6. Stable living, job, or economic situation.

Supporting Materials

- Dennis C. Daley, *Dual Diagnosis Workbook: Recovery Strategies for Addiction and Mental Health Problems*, Session 3, "Why I Came to Treatment," pp. 20–22; Session 6, "My Problem List and My Strengths," pp. 30–32. Independence, Missouri: Herald House/Independence Press, 1994.

PE GROUP #14
Setting Goals in Treatment
Of Dual Disorders

Objectives

- Clients learn the importance of setting goals in treatment.
- Clients learn the difference between short, medium, and long-term goals.
- Clients begin to prioritize goals that they want to achieve in treatment.
- Clients learn that reaching treatment goals requires active participation in a change plan.

Methods/Main Points

- Use lecture/discussion format. Write major points on a chalkboard or flip chart for reinforcement.

- Ask clients to discuss why it is important to set goals in relation to the problems that led to treatment for their dual disorders. Ask them to give some examples of treatment goals that they have set. Discuss the importance of setting goals in life, even if unrelated to dual recovery.

- Define short, medium, and long-term goals as follows:

  1. Short-term: less than three months

  2. Medium-term: four to twelve months

  3. Long-term: one year or longer

- Review the following important points about goals. Give concrete examples (elicit from clients or provide your examples) if necessary to illustrate these points:

  1. Goals are statements about what a person wants to achieve (e.g., to learn, do, accomplish, etc.). They imply action toward some end and are best described with action verbs.

  2. Goals provide structure and a mechanism to reach specific ends that are desirable.

  3. Goals are a way to judge whether one has made progress or reach a desired end.

  4. The process of working toward a goal may be just as important as the goal itself in some cases.

  5. It helps give a sense of direction in recovery if one sets specific goals.

- State the importance of having an "action plan" to follow to reach one's goals.

- Ask for examples of action plans clients have followed before in pursuing specific goals. Use these examples to illustrate how it helps to have several different coping strategies as part of an action plan rather than just one.

- Stress the importance of taking an active role in identifying and setting goals, developing action plans, and putting these plans into action if goals are to be achieved. Reinforce the importance of "walking the walk," not just "talking the talk" of recovery by setting and pursuing goals.

Supporting Materials

- Dennis C. Daley, *Dual Diagnosis Workbook: Recovery Strategies for Addiction and Mental Health Problems*. Session 7, "My Goals While I'm in Treatment," pp. 33–34. Independence, Missouri: Herald House/Independence Press, 1994.
- Dennis C. Daley, *Dual Diagnosis: Recovery Goal Checklist and Action Plan*.

PE GROUP #15
Advantages of Recovery From Dual Disorders

Objectives

- Clients learn that there are both advantages and disadvantages associated with giving up alcohol and drugs, and initiating a program of dual recovery.
- Client identify specific examples of advantages and disadvantages of giving up alcohol and other drugs.
- Identify advantages and disadvantages associated with involvement in a program of dual recovery.

Methods/Major Points

- Use lecture/discussion format. Write major points on a chalkboard or flip chart for reinforcement.
- State that there are both advantages and disadvantages associated with giving up alcohol and drugs, and initiating a program of recovery from addiction. Points to emphasize and discuss include:

    1. It is not easy to stop using chemicals and stay clean. A sense of "loss" or "grief" commonly accompanies abstinence.

    2. Most clients, especially in early recovery, have mixed feelings or ambivalence about sobriety.

    3. It is important to acknowledge that one has an "addicted side" that wants to continue using alcohol or other drugs.

    4. Acknowledging this reality first helps the client become able to focus on the advantages of giving up alcohol or drugs.

- Ask clients to respond to these points and to provide specific examples of disadvantages of giving up alcohol and other drugs. Discuss what they will miss most about not using chemicals.
- State there are many positive aspects, or advantages, of becoming sober or clean. These include, but are not limited to, positive changes in:

    1. Physical health

    2. Emotional health

    3. Family and social relationships

    4. Ability to work or attend school

5. Self-esteem

6. Spiritual health

7. Financial situation

- Teach client that similarly, there are advantages and disadvantages associated with involvement in a program of dual recovery. Some points to emphasize and discuss include:

  1. Recovery requires patience, discipline, and hard work.

  2. Recovery has rough spots; it is not always easy and at times one may want to give up or question one's ability to change.

  3. Although there are disadvantages, they should be outweighed by the many potential advantages of recovery.

- Have clients give personal examples of advantages that they have already experienced or expect to experience as dual recovery progresses.

Supporting Materials

- Dennis C. Daley, *Dual Diagnosis Workbook: Recovery Strategies for Addiction and Mental Health Problems*. Session 8, "Advantages of Recovery," pp. 35–37. Independence, Missouri: Herald House/Independence Press, 1994.

PE GROUP #16
Denial in Addiction and Psychiatric Illness

Objectives

- Clients learn to understand the psychological defense of denial in addiction and psychiatric illness.

- Identify specific ways in which denial of illness shows.

- Identify effects of denial.

- Clients are introduced to strategies used to break through the defense of denial in recovery.

Methods/Major Points

- Use lecture/discussion format. Write major points on a chalkboard or flip chart for reinforcement.

- Introduce the concept of psychological defenses that all people use. Give a few examples of various defense mechanisms, including denial. State that they are "unconscious" and occur out of our awareness.

- State that denial is commonly used with people who have addiction, psychiatric illness, or dual disorders. Denial is the refusal to believe or accept some painful reality in life and serves to protect a person from the anxiety associated with facing the truth about having a serious problem such as dual disorders.

- State that not only do clients use denial, but so do families and other people closely associated with them. Others also have difficulty accepting the reality of psychiatric illness, addiction, or both in a loved one.

- Give a few examples of denial in relation to psychiatric illness:

    1. Blaming problems on bad luck, bad break, or bad friends instead of acknowledging a psychiatric illness.

    2. Minimizing the seriousness of the psychiatric disorder (e.g., seeing oneself as having a bad case of the blues instead of a serious depressive illness).

    3. Refusing to believe one has a psychiatric illness because one holds a job, takes care of a family, or still functions fairly well in various areas of life.

    4. Blaming psychiatric symptoms on alcohol or other drugs.

- Ask clients to give personal examples of denial in relation to their psychiatric illness. Discuss why it is so difficult to accept psychiatric illness.

101

- Give a few examples of denial in relation to addiction:

   1. minimizing the problem because substances are not used every day or clients don't always lose control and get drunk or high when using chemicals;

   2. believing that alcohol/drug use is primarily caused by the psychiatric disorder;

   3. verbally acknowledging that an alcohol/drug problem exists, but outright refusing to do anything about it; and

   4. failure to accept abstinence as the best goal; agreeing to give up the main substance of abuse but continuing to use "other" substances (e.g., giving up cocaine or heroin, but continuing to use alcohol or marijuana).

- Ask clients to give additional personal examples of denial in addiction. Discuss why it is so difficult to accept addiction.

- Discuss some of the effects of denial of either or both disorders. Some examples include:

   1. ending up in the psychiatric hospital involuntarily;

   2. experiencing serious negative consequences of either or both disorders (health, legal, family, etc.); and

   3. inability to recover from one illness due to denial of symptoms of the other (e.g., psychiatric recovery gets complicated as a result of continued use of alcohol or other drugs).

- Discuss recovery strategies in relation to denial.

   1. Facing the facts of psychiatric illness by reviewing the symptoms, behaviors, and effects of illness on self and others. Stress the importance of knowing one's psychiatric diagnoses.

   2. Facing the facts of addiction by reviewing patterns of substance use, behaviors, and effects on self and others. Stress the importance of understanding the diagnoses.

   3. Getting specific feedback from health care professionals, family members, or other significant people regarding psychiatric symptoms or addictive symptoms observed over time.

Supporting Materials

- Dennis C. Daley, *Dual Diagnosis Workbook: Recovery Strategies for Addiction and Mental Health Problems.* Session 10, "Denial in Addiction and Psychiatric Illness," pp. 42–50. Independence, Missouri: Herald House/Independence Press, 1994.

- Merlene Miller, Terence T. Gorski, and David K. Miller, *Learning to Live Again: A Guide for Recovery from Chemical Dependency,* Updated and Revised Edition. Independence, Missouri: Herald House/Independence Press.

- Dennis C. Daley, *Working through Denial.* Minneapolis, Minnesota: Johnson Institute, 1990 (1-800-231-5165).

PE GROUP #17
Roadblocks in Recovery
From Dual Disorders

Objectives

- Clients learn that there are common roadblocks or barriers to dual recovery.
- Clients identify personal roadblocks to recovery.
- Clients begin to develop strategies to work through roadblocks so that they do not sabotage the recovery process.

Methods/Major Points

- Use lecture/discussion format. Write major points on the chalkboard or flip chart for reinforcement.
- State that there are many barriers and roadblocks that can interfere with ongoing recovery. These roadblocks can be classified into several categories (give an example or two for each category):
    1. Attitude and motivation roadblocks
    2. Personality roadblocks
    3. Personal relationship roadblocks
    4. Lifestyle roadblocks
- Review each category, asking clients to provide personal examples of their roadblocks. This can be done by eliciting examples from clients, or by reviewing the checklist of common roadblocks in the *Dual Diagnosis Workbook: Recovery Strategies for Addiction and Mental Health Problems.*
- Emphasize that awareness of personal roadblocks puts the client in a position to begin working through them.
- Ask clients to verbally identify one roadblock and list specific ways they can work through this roadblock. Or you can ask clients to fill in the section of the *Dual Diagnosis Workbook: Recovery Strategies for Addiction and Mental Health Problems* that asks for a specific roadblock and plan to overcome it.
- Emphasize commonalities in these recovery roadblocks and positive coping strategies. Add additional coping strategies to ones provided by clients as the discussion unfolds.

Supporting Materials

- Dennis C. Daley, *Dual Diagnosis Workbook: Recovery Strategies for Addiction and Mental Health Problems.* Session 11, "Roadblocks to Recovery," pp. 51–54.
- Videotape: *How to Sabotage Your Treatment.* Gerald T. Rogers Productions (1-800-227-9100).

PE GROUP #18
Recovery from Dual Disorders

Objectives

- Clients learn the importance of addressing both disorders in recovery.
- Recovery is emphasized as a process that involves abstinence + change + specific treatments.
- Introduce recovery as comprised of: motivation + information + skills + a program of change (professional treatment and self-help).
- Identify examples of physical, psychological, family, interpersonal, social, and spiritual aspects of recovery.
- Identify benefits of recovery.

Methods/Major Points

- Use a lecture/discussion format. Write major points on a chalkboard or flip chart for reinforcement.
- Ask clients to define recovery. Discuss recovery as a long-term "process" that involves abstinence from chemicals, change in coping strategies, and change in lifestyle. Specific types of treatment are needed, depending on the psychiatric disorder(s) clients are experiencing.

    1. Therapy—there are a number of different therapies for addiction, psychiatric illness, or both such as interpersonal, supportive, cognitive behavioral, dual disorders counseling, relapse prevention, and skills training.

    2. Family treatment

    3. Special programs—day hospital or intensive outpatient programs that involve combination treatments (individual, group, and social activities)

    4. Medications

    5. Self-help programs

- Emphasize the need to develop "internal" motivation for long-term recovery and progress.
- Ask clients to list some of the changes they think they need to make. Elaborate on their answers to provide the broad framework that recovery involves several areas of change:

    1. Physical
    2. Psychological
    3. Interpersonal
    4. Family
    5. Spiritual
    6. Financial

- Ask clients to dicuss the length of time they think they need to stay involved in professional treatment and/or self-help programs. Emphasize the importance of dealing both with short-term and long-term recovery issues.
- Ask clients to identify potential benefits of recovery in the following areas.

    1. Physical and medical

    2. Psychological and emotional

    3. Family

    4. Social and interpersonal

    5. Spiritual

    6. Legal

    7. Occupational

    8. Financial

Supporting Materials

- Dennis C. Daley, *Dual Diagnosis Workbook: Recovery Strategies for Addiction and Mental Health Problems.* Session 12, "Recovery from Dual Disorders," pp. 55–65. Independence, Missouri: Herald House/Independence Press, 1994.

- Dennis C. Daley, *Surviving Addiction Workbook: Practiced Tips on Developing a Recovery Plan.* Sections 5–11, pp. 9–22. Holmes Beach, Florida: Learning Publications, 1990 (1-800-222-1525).

- Dennis C. Daley and F. Campbell, *Coping with Dual Disorders: Chemical Dependency and Mental Illness,* 2nd ed. Center City, Minnesota: Hazelden, 1993 (1-800-328-9000).

PE GROUP #19
Coping with Cravings for
Alcohol or Drugs

Objectives

- Define cues, triggers or precipitants of alcohol/drug craving.
- Clients learn to identify their own external and internal precipitants of cravings.
- Clients learn to identify and label cravings.
- Clients learn practical skills to manage cravings.

Methods/Major Points

- Use a lecture/discussion format. Write the major points on a chalkboard or flip chart for reinforcement.

- Ask clients to define and describe an alcohol or drug craving. Then ask clients to identify factors that trigger their drug/alcohol cravings. Discuss precipitants as falling into one of two broad categories:

  1. Internal factors (feelings, thoughts)

  2. External factors (people, places, events, things)

- Have clients state ways their craving shows in:

  1. behaviors;

  2. thoughts; and

  3. physical symptoms.

- Have clients discuss various levels of intensity of cravings (from mild to very severe). State that the level of craving will determine coping strategies to use.

- State that clients should use multiple strategies to manage cravings because one strategy may not work effectively in every instance of a craving. Review coping strategies to manage alcohol/drug cravings:

  1. Recognition and labeling of craving

  2. Talking about the craving

  3. Going to a self-help meeting

  4. Talking oneself through the craving

5. Accepting that the craving will pass
6. Redirecting activity to distract oneself
7. Writing thoughts and feelings in a journal
8. Getting rid of booze, drugs, and paraphernalia
9. Avoiding high-risk people, places, and things
10. Praying or use of a Higher Power
11. Reading recovery literature

Supporting Materials

- Dennis C. Daley, *Dual Diagnosis Workbook: Recovery Strategies for Addiction and Mental Health Problems*. Session 13, "Coping with Cravings to Use Alcohol or Drugs," pp. 66–70. Independence, Missouri: Herald House/Independence Press, 1994.
- Dennis C. Daley, *Living Sober: An Interactive Video Recovery Program—Client Workbook*, 1994, pp. 6–8. Skokie, Illinois: Gerald T. Rogers Productions (1-800-227-9100).
- Videotape: *Living Sober: Coping with Cravings and Thoughts of Using*. Skokie, Illinois: Gerald T. Rogers Productions, 1994 (1-800-227-9100).

Coping with High-Risk People, Places, and Things

Objectives

- Define the concept of "high-risk people, places, and things" as it relates to recovery from dual disorders.
- Clients identify their own high-risk people, places, and things.
- Clients begin to identify strategies to help them cope with high-risk people, places, and things.

Methods/Major Points

- Use lecture/discussion format. Write major points on a chalkboard or flip chart for reinforcement.
- State that all clients have "high-risk people, places, and things" that can threaten recovery if they are unprepared. Although they may think of these mainly in relation to their addiction, the concept of high-risk people, places, and things can also be applied to recovery from psychiatric illness.
- In relation to addiction, high-risk people, places, and things are sometimes referred to as "triggers" because they precipitate cravings for alcohol or other drugs or increase the client's vulnerability to using chemicals.
- Ask clients for specific examples and add to their list as needed to cover a broad range of high-risk people, places and things that can threaten their recovery from addiction, psychiatric illness, or both. Common examples include:

  1. associating with drug dealers, other active addicts, or others who use drugs or get high on alcohol, even if they aren't addicted;

  2. living with a spouse or partner who gets high on alcohol or other drugs or has an addiction;

  3. maintaining a relationship with a significant other who is violent, extremely critical, or unable to have a mutual "give and take" relationship;

  4. spending time at places or events where alcohol or drugs flow freely (e.g., parties, bars, crack houses, etc.);

  5. associating sex with getting high or being unable to have sex unless high on drugs or alcohol; and

  6. other places and things that trigger desire to use chemicals, including music, drug paraphernalia, money, the sight or smell of other chemicals, positive thoughts of getting high, certain sexual partners, etc.

- Ask clients to state ways they can cope with high-risk people, places, and things. Add to their list of coping strategies as needed in order to ensure a variety of strategies are reviewed:

  1. avoiding high-risk people, places, and things;

  2. preparing ahead of time how to cope with a high-risk situation that cannot be avoided;

  3. ending relationships that are abusive or emotionally damaging;

  4. minimizing time spent with family members or significant others who are very critical or nonsupportive of recovery;

  5. requesting mates or partners with significant problems that represent a risk to the client's recovery to get involved in treatment; and

  6. gaining interpersonal strength to deal with destructive relationships through ongoing involvement in counseling.

- Review strategies to cope with alcohol or drug cravings that are triggered by high-risk people, places or things:

  1. talking oneself though the craving;

  2. accepting that it will eventually pass;

  3. distracting oneself and keeping busy;

  4. practicing relaxation or breathing;

  5. praying;

  6. getting physical exercise; and

  7. talking to a support person.

Supporting Materials

- Dennis C. Daley, *Living Sober: An Interactive Video Recovery Program—Client Workbook.* Section 2, "Resisting Social Pressures to Use Chemicals," and Section 3, "Coping with Cravings and Thoughts of Using." Skokie, Illinois: Gerald T. Rogers Productions, 1994 (1-800-227-9100).

- Dennis C. Daley, *Relapse Prevention Workbook: For Recovering Alcoholics and Drug Dependent Persons.* Section 3, "Identifying High-Risk Situations," pp. 4–7; Section 4, "Strategies to Handle High-Risk Situations," pp. 7–9. Holmes Beach, Florida: Learning Publications, 1986 (1-800-222-1525).

- Videotapes from Gerald T. Rogers Productions (Skokie, Illinois: 1-800-227-9100): *Living Sober: Resisting Social Pressures to Use Chemicals* (1994); *Living Sober: Coping with Cravings and Thoughts of Using Chemicals* (1994); *Staying Sober, Keeping Straight* (1988).

Coping with Persistent Symptoms
Of Psychiatric Illness

Objectives

- Define "persistent" or "chronic" symptoms of psychiatric illness.
- Clients can identify ways to monitor persistent or chronic symptoms in order to note any significant worsening of symptoms.
- Identify strategies to cope with persistent symptoms of psychiatric illness.

Methods/Major Points

- Use lecture/discussion format. Write major points on a chalkboard or flip chart for reinforcement.
- State that many psychiatric disorders, especially those considered recurrent, persistent, or chronic, are "lifelong conditions." Clients may experience some symptoms more or less continuously. These are called persistent or chronic symptoms.
- Ask clients for specific examples and add to their list as needed to generate a list of some common persistent mood, thinking, personality, or behavioral symptoms associated with various psychiatric illnesses:

    1. mood symptoms (e.g., anxiety, fear or worry, depression, emptiness, chronic anger, mania);

    2. thoughts symptoms (e.g., hallucinations, delusions, or loose associations); and

    3. personality or behavior symptoms (e.g., impulsivity, self-destructive or suicidal behaviors, aggressiveness or angry outbursts, emptiness, obsessions, compulsions, avoidance, antisocial behavior, etc.)

- State that some clients need to learn to live with persistent symptoms as they may never go away totally. The key is not whether or not the symptom is present, but the degree to which it is present and how it affects the client. For example, many clients will have to live with a certain amount of depression or anxiety. However, once these symptoms worsen significantly, other interventions may be needed.
- Discuss the importance of completing a daily inventory of select persistent symptoms so that clients can regularly monitor their symptoms. When target symptoms go beyond baseline or what clients can comfortably tolerate, different strategies need to be implemented.
- Show clients how to identify and rate persistent symptoms using the "Daily Symptom and Problem Checklist."
- Discuss when clients should ask for additional help from their counselor, treatment team, or sponsor:

1. When they or others are concerned about acting on suicidal or violent feelings.

2. When the level of personal suffering becomes high or intolerable.

3. When their symptoms interfere significantly with the ability to take care of basic needs or function.

4. When they think they have done all they can do to fight off the symptom.

Supporting Materials

- Dennis C. Daley, *Preventing Relapse*, pp. 12. "Daily Symptom and Problem Checklist." Center City, Minnesota: Hazelden, 1993 (1-800-328-9000).

- R. Liberman, *Social and Independent Living Skills: Patient Workbook*. "Coping with Persistent Symptoms," pp. 57–73, Los Angeles, California: UCLA Department of Psychiatry, 1988.

Coping with Anger
Part 1

Objectives

- Clients learn to define components of anger (feelings, thoughts, behaviors).
- Clients differentiate between healthy anger and methods of expression, and unhealthy anger and methods of expression.
- Identify the possible connections between feelings of anger and alcohol/drug use.
- Identify the possible connections between anger and psychiatric symptoms.
- Clients better understand the influence of early role models on the development of strategies used to cope with angry feelings.

Methods/Major Points

- Use a lecture and discussion format. Write the major points on a chalkboard or flip chart for reinforcement.
- Ask clients to give their definitions of anger. Relate their answers to the idea of anger having several different components:

  1. Emotional (feelings)

  2. Cognitive (thoughts and beliefs)

  3. Behavior (actions)

- State that we learn about anger from what we observe in early life, especially from parents or caretakers. Ask clients what they learned from their parents or caretakers about anger and its expression.
- State that anger can be healthy or unhealthy, depending on how it affects clients and how it is dealt with. Ask for examples of how anger shows in unhealthy and healthy attitudes and behaviors.

  1. Unhealthy

     - Acting out behaviors toward other people

     - Self-destructive behavior

     - Passivity or doing nothing and letting anger build up

     - Passive-aggressive behavior

2. Healthy

  • Expressing it when appropriate

  • Using anger to motivate oneself to solve a problem or accomplish something positive

• Ask clients to describe the connection between feelings of anger and alcohol and drug use.

  1. Using chemicals to control anger and desire to act out

  2. Using chemicals to give permission to let anger out

• Ask clients to give examples of the connection beween angry feelings and psychiatric or inter-personal problems.

  1. Depression

  2. Anxiety

  3. Low self-esteem

  4. Unsatisfying or conflictual relationships

Supporting Materials

• Dennis C. Daley, *Dual Diagnosis Workbook: Recovery Strategies for Addiction and Mental Health Problems*. Session 14, "Coping with Anger," pp. 72–77. Independence, Missouri: Herald House/Independence Press, 1994.

• Dennis C. Daley, *Coping with Anger Workbook*. Sections 1–3, pp. 3–14. Skokie, Illinois: Gerald T. Rogers Productions, 1991 (1-800-227-9100).

• Videotapes from Gerald T. Rogers Productions (1-800-227-9100): *Why Are You So Angry?* (1991); *Living Sober: Managing Anger in Recovery* (1994).

PE GROUP #23

Coping with Anger
Part 2

Objectives

- Clients learn that there are a number of coping strategies to manage angry feelings; some are healthy and some are unhealthy.

- Clients evaluate current coping strategies and views of how to handle anger, and the effects of these coping strategies on self and others.

- Review the benefits of learning how to cope with anger in positive ways.

- Identify coping strategies to handle anger (verbal, cognitive, and behavioral).

- Clients learn the importance of being able to cope with anger expressed by other people.

Methods/Major Points

- Use a lecture/discussion format, write the major points on a chalkboard or flip chart.

- Have clients give personal examples of ways they cope with anger.

    1. Unhealthy coping strategies

    2. Healthy coping strategies

- Have clients provide examples of some of the different effects of various coping strategies on self and others.

    1. Emotional effects

    2. Physical effects

    3. Interpersonal effects

- Review specific positive coping strategies for coping with anger and elicit examples from clients for each of the following categories:

    1. Verbal strategies

    2. Cognitive or self-talk strategies

    3. Behavioral strategies

- Review the eight-step process that can be used to cope with angry feelings.

    1. Step 1—Recognize and label feelings

    2. Step 2—Be aware of how feelings show

    3. Step 3—Look for causes of feelings

    4. Step 4—Evaluate the effects of feelings and coping style, both on oneself and other people

    5. Step 5—Identify coping strategies to deal with feelings

    6. Step 6—Rehearse or practice new coping strategies

    7. Step 7—Put new coping strategies into action

    8. Step 8—Change coping strategies as needed based on your evaluation of whether or not they were effective

- Identify concerns of clients related to coping with anger expressed by others.
- Discuss strategies to cope with other peoples' expression of anger.

Supporting Materials

- Dennis C. Daley, *Dual Diagnosis Workbook: Recovery Strategies for Addiction and Mental Health Problems*. Session 14, "Coping with Anger," pp. 72–77. Independence, Missouri: Herald House/Independence Press, 1994.
- Dennis C. Daley, *Coping with Anger Workbook*. Section 4, pp. 15–26. Skokie, Illinois: Gerald T. Rogers Productions, 1991 (1-800-227-9100).
- Videotapes from Gerald T. Rogers Productions (1-800-227-9100): *Why Are You So Angry?* (1991); *Living Sober: Managing Anger in Recovery* (1994).

PE GROUP #24
Coping with Anxiety and Worry

Objectives

- Define anxiety, worry, and anticipatory anxiety.

- Review causes of anxiety and worry.

- Clients learn that anxiety is a common problem with the chemically dependent, depressed individuals, and those with anxiety disorders.

- Identify how alcohol/drug use can increase or worsen anxiety.

- Clients learn that anxiety levels often increase when first stopping alcohol or other drugs (for physical and psychological reasons).

Methods/Major Points

- Use a lecture/discussion format. Write the major points on a chalkboard or flip chart for reinforcement.

- Ask clients to define anxiety and worry. Discuss how the two go together and how severe anxiety can lead to avoidant behavior.

  1. Anxiety = the physical side
  2. Worry = the psychological side

- Ask clients to identify reasons (causes) for anxiety and worry. Add additional examples as needed to cover the following broad categories of causes:

  1. Physiological
  2. Psychological
  3. Interpersonal

- Ask clients to identify and discuss the effects of anxiety and worry on:

  1. Physical health
  2. Emotional health
  3. Relationships

- Ask clients to state how alcohol and drug use may contribute to anxiety or make it worse (even if in the short-term, alcohol and drugs provide some temporary relief from anxiety).

- Review coping strategies for dealing with anxiety and worry (cognitive and behavioral):
    1. Identify and label anxiety and worry
    2. Find out what is causing anxiety and worry
    3. Get a physical examination
    4. Evaluate and change diet (especially use of caffeine)
    5. Evaluate lifestyle to identify sources of stress
    6. Meditate
    7. Use relaxation techniques
    8. Practice proper breathing techniques
    9. Change beliefs or thoughts
    10. Share anxious feelings and thoughts with others
    11. Set aside "worry time" each day
    12. Keep a written anxiety-and-worry journal
    13. Face the situations causing anxiety and worry

Supporting Materials

- Dennis C. Daley, *Dual Diagnosis Workbook: Recovery Strategies for Addiction and Mental Health Problems*. Session 15, "Coping with Anxiety and Worry," pp. 78-83. Independence, Missouri: Herald House/Independence Press, 1994.
- I. Salloum and Dennis C. Daley, *Understanding Major Anxiety Disorders and Addiction*. Center City, Minnesota: Hazelden, 1994 (1-800-328-9000).
- Videotapes:

    - *Double Trouble: Coping with Chemical Dependency and Mental Health Disorders. Part I—Mood and Anxiety Disorders and Addiction.* Gerald T. Rogers Productions (1-800-227-9100).

    - *Understanding Major Anxiety Disorders and Addiction.* Hazelden (1-800-328-9000).

PE GROUP #25
Coping with Boredom

Objectives

- Identify ways that boredom can impact relapse.
- Clients understand the importance of structure and routine in life to help reduce boredom and depression.
- Identify sources of boredom and high-risk times (times of the day, days of the week).
- Identify ways to build structure into day-to-day life.
- Clients are introduced to the idea of using a daily and/or weekly schedule of activities.

Methods

- Use lecture/discussion format. Write major points on a chalkboard or flip chart for reinforcement.
- Ask clients to identify and discuss how boredom can affect recovery from their dual disorders. Common problems associated with boredom include:

    1. going back to using alcohol or drugs;

    2. feeling depressed; and

    3. getting involved in activities or relationships that may temporarily reduce boredom but create serious problems later.

- Ask clients to discuss how they feel about "living without alcohol or drugs, or partying." Identify and list leisure activities given up due to addiction and recovery.
- Ask clients to identify non-alcohol/drug activities or situations that bring them pleasure or a sense of fun.
- Ask clients to identify and discuss the potential benefits of having a plan to build structure into their days and weeks.
- Review practical coping strategies to reduce boredom.

    1. Recognize boredom and determine the reasons for it

    2. Regain "lost" activities

    3. Learn to appreciate the simple pleasures in life

    4. Develop new interests

    5. Build fun into day-to-day life

    6. Identify "high risk" times for feeling bored

7. Change thoughts about boredom

8. Carefully evaluate relationship or job boredom before making any major changes

9. Deal with persistent feelings of boredom

10. Participate in support groups or recovery clubs

- Optional: Have clients complete a daily or weekly activities schedule to get them to practice building structure into their lives.

- Optional: Discuss the issue of "emptiness" and "joylessness" associated with giving up chemicals and how this contributes to both boredom and an inability to experience pleasure in normal activities.

Supporting Materials

- Dennis C. Daley, *Dual Diagnosis Workbook: Recovery Strategies for Addiction and Mental Health Problems.* Session 16, "Coping with Boredom," pp. 84–88. Independence, Missouri: Herald House/Independence Press, 1994.

- Dennis C. Daley, *Relapse Prevention Workbook: For Recovering Alcoholics and Drug Dependent Persons.* Section 8, "Use of Leisure Time in Sobriety," pp. 15–17. Holmes Beach, Florida: Learning Publications, 1981 (1-800-222-1525).

- Dennis C. Daley, *Living Sober: An Interactive Video Recovery Program—Client Workbook.* Section 5, pp. 12–14. Skokie, Illinois: Gerald T. Rogers Productions, 1994 (1-800-227-9100).

- Videotape: *Living Sober: Managing Feelings of Boredom and Emptiness.* Gerald T. Rogers Productions (1-800-227-9100).

Coping with Depression
Part 1

Objectives

- Clients learn to differentiate between depression as a clinical disorder and normal feelings of depression that most people experience at times.

- Identify symptoms of depressive illness.

- Clients learn about depression illness as a biopsychosocial disorder.

- Identify the possible relationships between alcohol and drug abuse and symptoms of depression.

- Clients understand the various causes of depressive illness.

Methods/Major Points

- Use a lecture/discussion format. Write the major points on a chalkboard or flip chart.

- Ask the clients to define depression.

- Ask the clients what they think is the difference between depression as a clinical disorder that brought them into treatment and normal feelings of depression that most people experience on occasion.

- Have clients give examples of symptoms of depressive illness they have experienced. Review the following symptoms of depressive illness:

    1. Feeling depressed or sad

    2. Trouble experiencing pleasure

    3. Appetite disturbance

    4. Sleep disturbance

    5. Feeling agitated or irritable

    6. Feeling slowed down

    7. Difficulty concentrating or remembering things

    8. Feeling helpless, hopeless, or guilty

    9. Loss or decrease in sexual desire

    10. Suicidality (thoughts of taking life, making a plan or making an actual attempt)

- State that clinical depression is characterized by multiple symptoms that are persistent and last several weeks or longer. Functioning is often impaired as a result.

- Have clients identify all the factors they think contributed to their depression. Use this to discuss different biopsychosocial factors involved in the development and maintenance of a depressive illness.

  1. Biological

  2. Psychological

  3. Environmental

  4. Interpersonal

- Have clients give examples of how their alcohol/drug use affected their depressed mood. State that both acute and chronic effects of drugs, or withdrawal states, can cause symptoms of depression.

- Have clients give examples of how depressed mood may impact their decision to use alcohol or other drugs.

Supportive Materials

- Dennis C. Daley, *Dual Diagnosis Workbook: Recovery Strategies for Addiction and Mental Health Problems.* Session 17, "Coping with Depression," pp. 89–95. Independence, Missouri: Herald House/Independence Press, 1994.

- M. Thase and Dennis C. Daley, *Understanding Depression and Addiction.* Center City, Minnesota: Hazelden, 1994 (1-800-328-9000).

- Videotapes:

  - *Double Trouble: Coping with Chemical Dependency and Mental Health Disorders—Part I, Mood and Anxiety Disorders and Addiction.* Gerald T. Rogers Productions (1-800-227-9100.

  - *Understanding Depression and Addiction.* Hazelden (1-800-328-9000).

PE GROUP #27
Coping with Depression
Part 2

Objectives

- Identify different types of clinical depression.
- Clients learn about the various professional treatments used for depressive illness.
- Review strategies that clients can use to help them cope with symptoms of depression.
- Identify the effects of continued alcohol and drug use on depressive illness and recovery from it.
- Identify the effects of drinking alcohol or using other drugs on medications used to treat depressive illness.

Methods/Major Points

- Use a lecture/discussion format. Write the major points on a chalkboard or flip chart.
- Review the different types of depressive illness:

    1. Single major depressive episode
    2. Seasonal
    3. Dysthymia
    4. Recurrent depression
    5. Manic-depressive illness

- Emphasize the importance of ongoing involvement in treatment and recovery for recurrent conditions, as well as for manic depressive illness.
- Tell clients that a variety of specific treatments have been effectively used with depressive illness. It is one of the most treatable psychiatric conditions. These include the use of psychotherapies and medication or the two used in combination. Then, review the goals of psychotherapy and medication in relation to depression.

    1. Improve specific symptoms of the mood disorder
    2. Increase positive thinking and decrease negative thinking
    3. Improve functioning
    4. Improve self-esteem
    5. Learn to live with persistent symptoms of depression

- Ask clients how they think continuing to drink alcohol or use drugs will affect their recovery from depressive illness. Discuss how use of chemicals can:

    1. temporarily mask depressive symptoms;
    2. increase depressive symptoms;
    3. decrease motivation to recover; and
    4. interfere with ability to make changes in self, lifestyle, or coping mechanisms

- Ask clients to state examples of how drinking and drug use affect the effectiveness of psychiatric medications.

    1. Can raise level in blood
    2. Can lower level in blood

- Ask clients to identify strategies to cope with symptoms of depressive illness. Review the following strategies:

    1. Find out the problems that are contributing to depression and do something about them.
    2. Evaluate relationships with other people.
    3. Make amends.
    4. Keep active.
    5. Talk about feelings and problems with others.
    6. Look for other emotions or feelings that may contribute to, or be associated with, depression (e.g., guilt, anger, emptiness).
    7. Change depressed thoughts.
    8. Focus on positive things.
    9. Keep a journal or "depression log."
    10. Participate in pleasant activities each day.
    11. Identify and plan future activities that one can look forward to enjoying.
    12. Participate in depression recovery support groups.
    13. Take medications as prescribed.

Supportive Materials

- Dennis C. Daley, *Dual Diagnosis Workbook: Recovery Strategies for Addiction and Mental Health Problems.* Session 17, "Coping with Depression," pp. 89–95. Independence, Missouri: Herald House/Independence Press, 1994.
- M. Thase and Dennis C. Daley, *Understanding Depression and Addiction.* Center City, Minnesota: Hazelden (1-800-328-9000).
- Videotapes:

  Double Trouble: Coping with Chemical Dependncy and Mental Health Disorders. Part I — Mood and Anxiety Disorders and Addiction. Gerald T. Rogers Productions (1-800-227-9100).

  Understanding Depression and Addiction. Hazelden (1-800-328-9000).

PE GROUP #28
Coping with Guilt and Shame

Objectives

- Define "guilt" and "shame."
- Clients begin to share feelings of guilt and shame, and specific experiences for which they feel guilty (can relate to addiction and/or psychiatric illness).
- Relate alcohol and drug use to behaviors associated with feeling guilty and shameful.
- Clients learn that that failure to deal with guilt and shame may increase vulnerability to relapse.
- Identify methods to begin coping with guilt and shame.
- Discuss the importance of "changing behaviors" and "making amends" if these feeling of guilt and shame are to be worked through.

Methods/Major Points

- Use a lecture/discussion format. Write the major points on a chalkboard or flip chart for reinforcement.
- State that feelings of guilt and shame are common among people with psychiatric illness, addiction, or dual disorders.
- Have clients give their definitions of guilt and shame. Differentiate them as follows:

  1. Guilt—feeling bad about one's behaviors (actions or inactions).

  2. Shame—feeling bad about oneself ("I'm defective," "I'm weak," "I'm a failure for having an addiction or psychiatric illness").

- Have clients state the reasons they feel guilty or shameful. Encourage them to talk about what it feels like to have dual disorders as well as some of the things they have done or failed to do that contribute to guilt.
- Reframe "shame" and talk about addiction and psychiatric disorders as "no-fault illnesses." Emphasize one did not purposely set out to acquire any of these illnesses. However, it is important that clients accept responsibility to change and get well.
- Discuss coping strategies (professional help and self-help programs) for working through guilt and shame.

  1. Recognize feelings of guilt and shame.

  2. Take time to work through guilt and shame.

  3. Accept limitations and accept dual disorders as "no-fault" illnesses.

  4. Share feelings of guilt and shame.

  5. Use the Twelve-Step program.

124

6. Make amends to others hurt by the dual disorders.

7. Seek forgiveness from others.

8. Pray and seek help from a Higher Power.

Supporting Materials

- Dennis C. Daley, *Coping with Feelings Workbook*. Section 13, "Guilt and Shame Analysis," and Section 14, "Review of Strategies for Coping with Guilt and Shame," pp. 45–51. Holmes Beach, Florida: Learning Publications, 1994 (1-800-222-1525).
- Twelve-Step handouts.

PE GROUP #29
Sharing Positive Feelings in Recovery

Objectives

- Discuss the importance of experiencing and expressing positive feelings.
- Identify positive feelings that one can experience.
- Identify strategies for sharing positive feelings and potential benefits to relationships of sharing such feelings.

Methods/Major Points

- Use lecture/discussion format. Write major points on a chalkboard or flip chart for reinforcement.

- State that although much discussion in recovery focuses on coping with negative feelings such as anger, guilt, or depression, it is also important to focus on positive feelings. Similar to other feelings, these also show in behaviors and what is said to others. Stress that saying positive things without backing these up with actions will have limited impact. For example:

  1. A person can tell another, "I love you," but generally treat them very poorly. These words will have little impact as a result.

  2. A person can tell another, "I love you," and do nice things for this other person and show this love in their actions.

- Ask group members to share their thoughts on why it is important to experience and express positive feelings. Add to their ideas as needed and include some of the following examples of the potential benefits of sharing positive feelings:

  1. contributes to satisfaction in life;

  2. promotes better mental health;

  3. raises self-esteem;

  4. helps build better interpersonal relationships; and

  5. helps to balance out negative feelings in relationships.

- Ask group members to share some positive feelings that they have experienced and that they believe are important. Add to their examples as needed and cover a range of examples such as:

  1. Affection

  2. Hopefulness

  3. Love

  4. Joy

126

5. Caring

6. Glad

7. Happy

8. Passionate

9. Thankful

10. Playful

- Ask group members to identify ways positive feelings can be shared.

    1. In words—elicit specific examples

    2. In actions—elicit specific examples

Supporting Materials

- Dennis C. Daley, *Coping with Feelings Workbook*, Section 9, "Love and Recovery," and Section 10, "Expressing Positive Feelings," pp. 52–58. Holmes Beach, Florida: Learning Publications, 1994 (1-800-222-1525).

PE GROUP #30
Impact of Dual Disorders
On Relationships

Objectives

- Clients learn that family and interpersonal relationships are often negatively affected by behaviors associated with either or both disorders.
- Identify specific effects of dual disorders on clients' family, friends, coworkers, or others.
- Identify ways to begin repairing some of the damage done to family and other personal relationships.

Methods/Major Points

- Use lecture/discussion format. Write major points on a chalkboard or flip chart for reinforcement.
- State that relationships with family and others are often hurt by behaviors associated with substance use, psychiatric illness, or both. These negative effects range from mild to quite severe.
- Ask clients to provide examples of behaviors and adverse effects of their disorders on family or other significant people in their lives. Add to this list as needed in order to provide a broad overview of various behaviors and adverse interpersonal effects of dual disorders. Some examples to cover include:

  1. broken or lost relationships;
  2. distrust from others;
  3. lying, stealing, or conning others, especially in relation to getting or using substances or covering-up use;
  4. emotional upset (anger, disappointment, confusion, anxiety or worry, depression);
  5. an inability to take care of responsibilities toward others (e.g., cannot fulfill parental role, relate on mutual level with partner, provide for family, etc.); and
  6. emotional or physical violence toward others.

- State that an important aspect of recovery is repairing some of the damage caused in relationships. Ask clients to give examples of strategies they can use to begin improving relationships damaged by their disorders. Add additional ideas as needed to their list and cover the following strategies:

  1. inviting family or significant others to treatment sessions;
  2. encouraging family or significant others to attend self-help groups;
  3. providing information regarding dual disorders and recovery to family or significant others;

4. acknowledging that the family or others were affected by one's dual disorders;

5. openly discussing the impact of dual disorders on the family or significant others, allowing others to share what it was like for them; and

6. working Steps 8 and 9 of the AA, NA, CA, DRA, or EA program (making amends steps).

• Stress that verbal strategies to improve relationships will have little or no impact unless they are backed up by positive behavior change. For example, it does little good to apologize for verbal or physical aggression if one doesn't change these behaviors.

Supporting Materials

• Dennis C. Daley, *Improving Communication and Relationships.* Section 2, "Effects of Chemical Dependency on Friendships," and Section 3, "Making Amends." Holmes Beach, Florida: Learning Publications, 1995 (1-800-222-1525).

• Dennis C. Daley, *Surviving Addiction Workbook: Practical Tips on Developing a Recovery Plan.* Section 9, "Social Recovery," pp. 17–18. Holmes Beach, Florida: Learning Publications, 1990 (1-800-222-1525).

• Terence T. Gorski, *Getting Love Right*, Section 2, "Building a Healthy Relationship," pp. 133–226. New York: Simon & Schuster.

• Videotape: *Living Sober: Coping with Family and Interpersonal Conflicts.* Gerald T. Rogers Productions (1-800-227-9100).

PE GROUP #31
Dual Disorders and the Family

Objectives

- Clients learn that dual disorders can have a variety of effects on the family unit as well as individual members.

- Clients become aware of common concerns and questions of families related to dual diagnosis and recovery.

- Identify specific ways the addiction, mental health disorder, or both affected the clients' families.

- Clients recognize the importance of involving the family in the assessment and treatment processes.

- Clients recognize when a family member (e.g., a spouse or child) may need help with a mental health or addictive disorder.

Methods/Major Points

- Use lecture/discussion format. Write major points on a chalkboard or flip chart for reinforcement.

- State that addiction, mental illness, and dual disorders are associated with a number of family-related problems. Both the family unit and individual members may be affected, directly or indirectly, in a variety of different ways.

- State that effects of dual disorders on the family may vary from mild to severe, depending on a number of factors such as the severity of the addiction, behaviors of the dual disordered family member, and coping skills of family members.

- Ask clients to provide examples of how their family units and individual members were affected by the dual disorders.

- Expand on the list generated by clients to identify some additional ways families and members are affected by dual disorders. Try to give examples from the following general categories:

  1. Family mood and atmosphere
  2. Communication in the family
  3. Interactions between family members
  4. Emotional effects on family members (e.g., anger, depression, confusion, anxiety, etc.)
  5. Financial effects

130

- Discuss the importance of family involvement in assessment and treatment. Mention that there are a variety of types of sessions the family may attend (evaluation, education, counseling) and that family members' involvement can help in two general ways:

  1. supporting the dual diagnosed member's recovery; and

  2. gaining help and support for him/herself.

- Discuss the possibility that other family members may have serious psychiatric disorders or substance use disorders that require treatment. Discuss "red flags" for determining if a child or teenager may need professional help. Then discuss ways to go about getting this help. Problems that warrant a possible evaluation include:

  1. Severe anxiety

  2. Depression or mood swings

  3. Hearing voices or having very bizarre thoughts (e.g., that people are trying to put thoughts in or take them out of their heads)

  4. Becoming violent with other people

  5. Expressing thoughts of suicide

  6. Trouble concentrating or completing schoolwork, leading to poor grades

  7. Skipping school a lot

  8. Trouble getting along with other kids at home or school

  9. Trouble with the law

Supporting Materials

- Dennis C. Daley, *Dual Diagnosis Workbook: Recovery Strategies for Addiction and Mental Health Problems*. Section 17, "Your Family and Recovery," pp. 98–106. Independence, Missouri: Herald House/Independence Press, 1994.

- Dennis C. Daley and J. Sinberg, *A Family Guide to Dual Disorders* (2nd ed.). Center City, Minnesota: Hazelden, 1995 (1-800-328-9000).

- Videotape: *Double Trouble: Coping with Chemical Dependency and Mental Health Disorders. Part I—Mood and Anxiety Disorders and Addiction.* Story 1, "Depression," Story 2, "Anxiety." Gerald T. Rogers Productions (1-800-227-9100).

PE GROUP #32
Saying No to Getting High

Objectives

- Clients learn to anticipate direct and indirect social pressures to use alcohol or other drugs.
- Identify the effects of social pressures on thoughts, feelings, and behaviors.
- Clients learn about "relapse set-ups"— how they put themselves in high-risk social pressure situations (consciously or unconsciously).
- Identify coping strategies to deal with social pressures to use alcohol or other drugs.

Methods/Major Points

- Use lecture/discussion and role-play format. Write major ideas on a chalkboard or flip chart for reinforcement.
- Ask clients to identify examples of direct and indirect social pressures to use that they have faced or expect to face in the future. These will usually fall in one of these categories:

  1. People
  2. Places
  3. Events
  4. Situations

- Choose one or two common social pressure situations and set up role-plays in which *one client* is offered alcohol/drugs by another person. Ask other group members observing the role-play to identify with the client being offered alcohol or drugs, and to pay attention to their thoughts and feelings.

- After the role-play, process it with actors and the other group members. Focus on the following:

  1. What do clients feel when confronted by pressures to use?
  2. What thoughts come into their minds when offered alcohol or drugs?
  3. What can they do to cope?

- Optional: Have clients pair up in dyads. Each offers the other alcohol or drugs. After this experience, process it in group as in #4 above.

- Optional: Use a male/female in the role-play and instruct the individual offering alcohol or drugs to add discussion of a "good time" or sex. A male client might feel more vulnerable to an offer by a female to get high because of the association between sex and getting high with a woman (or vice versa).

- After the group processes the role-play, review coping strategies:

1. Avoidance of high-risk social pressure situations

2. Verbal (ways to say no)

3. Behavioral (ways to reduce or deal with unavoidable social pressures)

• Also, discuss the issue of "ambivalence," i.e., this role-play often helps clients see the part of them that still wants to get high and that "misses the action."

Supporting Materials

• Dennis C. Daley, *Dual Diagnosis Workbook: Recovery Strategies for Addiction and Mental Health Problems*. Session 19, "Saying No to Getting High," pp. 102–105. Independence, Missouri: Herald House/Independence Press, 1994.

• Dennis C. Daley, *Relapse Prevention Workbook*, "Identifying and Handling Social Pressures," pp. 10–13. Holmes Beach, Florida: Learning Publications (1-800-222-1525).

• Videotapes from Gerald T. Rogers Productions (1-800-227-9100): *Staying Sober, Keeping Straight* (1988). *Living Sober: Resisting Social Pressures to Use Chemicals* (1994).

PE GROUP #33
Coping with Pressures to Stop Taking Psychiatric Medications

Objectives

- Clients learn to anticipate pressures from others to stop taking their psychiatric medications.
- Identify effects of such pressures on their thoughts, feelings, and behaviors.
- Identify coping strategies to handle pressures to stop taking psychiatric medications.

Methods/Major Points

- Use lecture/discussion format. Write major points on a chalkboard or flip chart for reinforcement.
- Have group members give examples of past experiences in which they were pressured to stop taking medications (or have some typical scenarios available to role-play should clients be unable to provide examples). Common scenarios may include:

  1. a member of AA, NA, or CA tells a client that he/she is not really sober or clean because medications (drugs) are still being used;

  2. a family member or friend tells a client that he/she shouldn't be on medication; and

  3. a member of a support group, family member, or friend tells the client of their own "bad experiences" with psychiatric medications, and suggests that the client might want to reconsider the need for medications.

- Choose one or two of these situations and set up role-plays in which one client is told by another that he/she should stop taking psychiatric medications. Use the role-plays to demonstrate some of the issues related to pressures from others to stop taking medications. Ask clients observing the role-play to identify with the person being pressured to stop taking medicine and to pay close attention to what they think and feel.

- After the role-play, discuss the effects of such situations on the clients' thoughts, feelings, and behaviors. Focus on the factors involved in making a decision as to whether or not one will continue taking psychiatric medications or give in to pressure from others to stop.

- Ask clients to discuss the implications of stopping psychiatric medications. Reinforce the difference between drugs used to get high or drunk and those used to treat medical or psychiatric illnesses.

- Review positive coping strategies that clients can use to handle pressures to stop taking medications:

  1. Informing sponsor about being on medications

  2. Being discreet about who else is told about psychiatric medications

3. Telling the person pressuring the client to stop medicines that are needed for a medical problem

4. Reminding the person pressuring the client to stop, that the client may get sick again or even relapse to alcohol or drug use if medications are stopped

5. Asking the person if he/she makes the same request regarding medicines for a heart condition or other medical problem

6. Keeping in mind that only a doctor should tell clients when they should stop taking medications

7. Leaving the situation if the pressures become too great

- Optional: Have clients pair up in dyads. In each dyad, one client tells the other that he/she should consider getting off all drugs, including medications from "shrinks." Each client practices responding to this situation. Then the group as a whole discusses the experience, focusing on thoughts, feelings, and behaviors generated by such pressure. Both ineffective and positive coping strategies can be identified.

Supporting Materials

- *The AA Member, Medication and Other Drugs*. New York: AA World Services.
- 3 X 5 index cards with examples of common scenarios related to this topic.

Building a Recovery Network

Objectives

- Emphasize the importance of having a positive social support system (introduce term "recovery network").
- Clients become aware of common resistances and problems in building a recovery network (e.g., guilt, shame and embarrassment; inability to ask for help, etc.).
- Assess current social support systems to determine changes needed to support clients' ongoing efforts at recovery.
- Identify potential sources of support in recovery (individuals and organizations).
- Emphasize the importance of families/significant others getting involved in treatment and/or self-help programs.

Methods/Major Points

- Use a lecture/discussion format. Write the main points on a chalkboard or flip chart for reinforcement.
- Introduce the term "recovery network" and emphasize the importance of working a "We" recovery program versus an "I" program.
- Ask clients to identify people and organizations who could help support their efforts at recovery. They may include:

  1. Family
  2. Friends
  3. AA, NA, CA, DRA
  4. Mental health support groups
  5. Church
  6. Other organizations

- Ask clients to state specific ways others can help or support them. Some examples include:

  1. listening to problems or difficulties;
  2. offering advice;
  3. spending time in an enjoyable activity together;
  4. discussing ways to use the "tools" of recovery (especially true for sponsors and other members of support groups); and
  5. helping with some practical need (ride to a meeting, help moving furniture, etc.).

- Discuss the importance of "making amends" to others (especially family members and close friends) hurt by behaviors associated with either illness before asking for help and support.
- Ask clients to discuss the reasons why they might not ask for help, or why others may prefer not helping or supporting their recovery. Some examples include:

  1. feelings of guilt, shame, or embarrassment;

  2. afraid the other person will refuse;

  3. don't know what to say when asking from others; and

  4. others may still be very upset and angry at the client.

- Review strategies for asking for help. Use role-plays to illustrate the process of asking for help and to help the client become aware of how difficult this can be. Role-play can focus on concrete situations such as asking for a sponsor, asking someone to listen to a problem, or asking someone for a favor.
- Emphasize the need to work with others in recovery and to ask for help and support while still taking responsibility for recovery. Strongly emphasize the importance of AA/NA, dual recovery, and mental health support groups.

Supporting Materials

- Dennis C. Daley, *Dual Diagnosis Workbook: Recovery Strategies for Addiction and Mental Health Problems*. Session 20, "Developing and Using a Relapse Prevention Support System," pp. 109–110. Independence, Missouri: Herald House/Independence Press, 1994.
- Videotape: *Living Sober: Building a Recovery Network and Sponsorship*. Gerald T. Rogers Productions (1-800-227-9100).

PE GROUP #35
Self-Help Programs and Dual Recovery

Objectives

- Emphasize the importance of self-help programs in recovery.
- Provide information on various types of self-help programs for addiction (e.g., AA, NA, CA), psychiatric illness (Emotions Anonymous, support groups for specific types of psychiatric illness), and for dual disorders (e.g., Double Trouble, Dual Recovery Anonymous).
- Provide information on the "tools" of self-help programs (meetings, slogans, literature, etc.).
- Identify ways a "sponsor" can aid recovery.
- Stress the helpfulness of "recovery clubs."

Methods/Major Points

- Use lecture/discussion format. Write major points on a chalkboard or flip chart for reinforcement.
- Ask clients about their experiences in self-help groups—types of groups attended, specific ways they have been helpful, and objections or resistances to attending self-help groups.
- Review the different types of self-help groups for clients with dual disorders:

  1. AA, NA, CA, RR, WFS for addiction

  2. Emotions Anonymous, Recovery Inc., and other specific disorder based support groups (e.g., depression and manic-depressive support groups)

  3. Double Trouble, MISA, and DRA for dual disorders

- Review ways self-help groups can aid recovery.

  1. Providing information

  2. Getting help and support from others in recovery who have similar problems

  3. Getting exposure to the 12-Step program of recovery

  4. Having an opportunity to work with a sponsor

  5. Helping structure free time by involvement in recovery-oriented social activities

  6. Learning coping skills to deal with the various adjustments and problems associated with the dual disorders

- Review the role of a "sponsor" in recovery and how to go about getting one in AA, NA, CA, or other self-help programs.
- Review the different types and formats of self-help meetings:

1. Open discussion of recovery issues

2. Structured discussions (e.g., on one of the 12 Steps of AA/NA, on the "Big Book" of AA or "Basic Text" of NA)

3. Lead meetings in which a personal story of recovery is shared.

4. Guest speakers

5. Special meetings: for specific disorders; gender specific; groups for gays or lesbians, health-care professionals, business people, students, etc.

• Discuss the 12-Step program and how this can be used in ongoing recovery to address a variety of important recovery themes (e.g., making amends, identifying character defects, taking a daily inventory, etc.).

• Discuss the concept and purpose of "recovery clubs" and provide information on any local clubs.

• Review some of the other "tools of recovery":

1. Slogans

2. Literature

3. Use of a Higher Power

4. Serenity Prayer

• Reiterate that recovery is a "we" rather than an "I" endeavor and that much support is available for any person in dual recovery who is willing to use this support.

Supporting Materials

• Dennis C. Daley, *Dual Diagnosis Workbook: Recovery Strategies for Addiction and Mental Health Problems.* Session 21, "AA/NA, Mental Health Support Groups and Recovery Clubs," pp. 111–115. Independence, Missouri: Herald House/Independence Press, 1994.

• Copy of the Serenity Prayer, Slogans, 12-Steps of Recovery of AA/NA, or modified Steps for DRA or Double Trouble Groups, and/or local self-help meeting lists.

• Terence T. Gorski, *How to Start Relapse Prevention Support Groups.* Independence, Missouri: Herald House/Independence Press (1989).

• Videotape: *Living Sober: Building a Recovery Network and Sponsorship.* Gerald T. Rogers Productions (1-800-227-9100).

PE GROUP #36
Changing Self-Defeating Behaviors

Objectives

- Acquaint clients with common self-defeating behaviors associated with recovery from dual disorders.

- Acquaint clients with self-destructive behaviors associated with types of psychiatric illness and addiction.

- Clients learn to identify their own self-defeating and self-destructive behaviors.

- Clients learn to begin to look at ways of changing self-defeating and self-destructive behaviors.

Methods/Major Points

- Use a lecture/discussion format. Write the major points on a chalkboard or flip chart for reinforcement.

- Define self-defeating behaviors. These behaviors refer to involvement in activities that threaten the clients' emotional well-being or their relationships. Self-defeating behaviors also can adversely affect the client's financial status, ability to get or keep a job, or ability to function in other areas of life.

- Elicit some specific examples of self-defeating behaviors from clients. Then mention some of the following to provide concrete examples for them:

    1. Jumping from one relationship to the next

    2. Getting easily bored with a partner

    3. Moving in with a partner after knowing him/her for only a short period of time

    4. Picking up strangers and having sex with them

    5. Getting involved too quickly in a romantic relationship

    6. Getting involved in relationships that are physically or emotionally abusive

    7. Using intimidation and anger to keep people on their guard

    8. Quitting jobs impulsively

    9. Managing money poorly and getting deep in debt

    10. Gambling too much or compulsively

    11. Compulsive sexual behavior

    12. Getting involved in illegal activities or criminal behaviors

- Define self-destructive behaviors: behaviors that can cause great physical or psychological harm to the client or another person. Examples include:

    1. suicidal acts;

    2. physical self-destructive acts such as cutting or burning oneself;

    3. punching a wall;

    4. physical violence toward other people;

    5. breaking or destroying property; and

    6. overdosing on drugs.

- State that certain illnesses such as personality disorders or manic-depressive disorder often involve impulsive behavior that leads toward self-destructive or self-defeating behaviors.

- Some self-destructive or self-defeating behaviors caused by poor judgment during an episode of illness such as a manic or psychotic break may stop when the psychiatric illness is stabilized. However, this is not always the case.

- State that changing these behaviors first involves gaining an awareness of what they are and what causes them. This put clients in a better position to begin strategizing and devising action plans to reduce these harmful behaviors or stop them altogether.

- Have clients identify one self-defeating or self-destructive behavior they want to change. Have them talk about this briefly in the group session. Then elicit concrete examples from the group members. Also, have group members talk about ways they can change the self-defeating or self-destructive behaviors identified as problematic.

- Summarize some general strategies that may be used to change these behaviors. Use some of the examples of coping strategies given by group members. You can also add other strategies as well.

    1. Cognitive strategies

    2. Behavior strategies

    3. Personality change strategies

Supporting Materials

- Dennis C. Daley, *Dual Diagnosis Workbook: Recovery Strategies for Addiction and Mental Health Problems*. Session 22, "Changing Self-defeating and Self-destructive Behaviors," pp. 118–122. Independence, Missouri: Herald House/Independence Press, 1994.

PE GROUP #37
Changing Personality Problems

Objectives

- Define personality and personality problems.

- Clients learn to understand the connection between personality traits and problems, and addiction.

- Clients begin to identify specific problematic traits that may hinder their recovery or well-being.

- Clients begin to develop strategies to change one problematic personality trait identified.

Methods/Major Points

- Use a lecture/discussion format. Write the major points on a chalkboard or flip chart for reinforcement.

- Ask clients to define personality. After they have given some examples, define personality as a person's characteristic way of seeing the world and relating to other people. It shows in specific behaviors and patterns of relating to oneself and to other people.

- State that personality problems are fairly common among people with addictions. There are a couple of ways of looking at this:

    1. One way is to look at specific personality traits that cause problems but are not necessarily part of a specific personality disorder.

    2. Another way is to relate some of the more serious kinds of personality problems to specific psychiatric disorders such as borderline, antisocial, or dependent personality disorders.

- Elicit examples of problematic personality problems from clients and ask them to talk about ways these traits or problems have influenced drug and alcohol use, caused problems in their relationship with other people, or caused other suffering or personal distress in their life.

- Ask clients if they have heard the term "character defect" as used in 12-Step programs. Then ask them to define what they think it means and how they relate to it in terms of their own personality. Relate this concept to changing problematic personality traits as part of ongoing recovery. Stress that personality change tends to take a long time and doesn't happen overnight.

- Discuss the importance of seeing personality traits on a continuum and that even some that are identified as so-called negative or problematic may have positive aspects to them. Also, traits identified as positive can have negative aspects to them.

1. For example, aggressiveness can get one in trouble if it is used to hurt other people or to put other people down. However, aggressiveness can be very helpful in business situations, athletic situations, or situations where other people want to take advantage of the client.

2. Similarly, kindness can be a positive trait and help one develop solid reciprocal relationships. However, if one is too kind and always "giving to others" then they may harbor a resentment on the inside and may be dissatisfied in their interpersonal relationships as a result.

3. Therefore, it is usually not the trait in and of itself but the degree to which it affects the person in recovery that is important.

- Get each client to identify one trait that he/she would like to change and begin discussing ways to change this trait. Use these client examples to point out some common ways people change personality traits and problems over time. Emphasize that change requires practice.

    1. Change beliefs about the trait and associated behavior. For example, a client who is too passive and unable to express anger can work on changing the belief that "anger is bad and should be avoided at all costs" to "anger is a normal part of life."

    2. Change behavior associated with the trait. For example, a passive client can practice being more assertive and express ideas, thoughts, and feelings rather than hold these in.

Supporting Materials

- Dennis C. Daley, *Dual Diagnosis Workbook: Recovery Strategies for Addiction and Mental Health Problems.* Session 23, "Changing Personality Traits," pp. 123-126. Independence, Missouri: Herald House/Independence Press, 1994.
- R. Weiss and Dennis C. Daley, *Understanding Personality Problems and Addiction.* Center City, Minnesota: Hazelden, 1994 (1-800-328-9000).
- Videotape: *Double Trouble: Recovery from Chemical Dependency and Mental Illness. Part II—Personality Disorders.* Gerald T. Rogers Productions (1-800-227-9100).

PE GROUP #38
Changing Negative Thinking

Objectives

- Clients learn that beliefs and thoughts impact feelings and actions, and affect both recovery and relapse.

- Clients learn to identify common "cognitive distortions" that impact recovery and relapse of either disorder.

- Identify strategies to change cognitive distortions and challenge negative thinking.

- Introduce the concept of "stinking thinking" discussed in AA/NA programs.

Methods/Major Points

- Use a lecture/discussion format. Write the major points on a chalkboard or flip chart for reinforcement.

- Elicit examples of negative beliefs or statements, or "stinking thinking." Ask how these impact a client's feelings or behaviors. State that these have a great impact on clients' ability to cope with their disorders and life problems.

- Provide examples of cognitive distortions or other negative thoughts common among dual disordered clients. These include:

  1. Black-and-white thinking

  2. Making things worse than they are

  3. Overgeneralizing

  4. Expecting the worst to happen

  5. Ignoring the positive and focusing on the negative

  6. Jumping to conclusions

- Review a three-step process of challenging cognitive distortions and negative thinking.

  Step 1—identify the belief or thought.

  Step 2—state what is faulty or incorrect about it.

  Step 3—come up with two to four counterstatements for each belief or thought.

- Have clients identify specific examples of their thinking to practice using these three steps. Have several clients share their examples in group to illustrate the main points of this session. Other clients can add additional ideas on counterstatements for the examples shared.

- Discuss the importance of small changes. For example, if a client can reduce negative thinking by 10 percent this is good progress. Clients should not expect major changes to occur quickly. Cognitive changes require practice over and over again.

- Encourage clients to continue their work by practicing changing thoughts and beliefs between group sessions.

Supporting Materials

- Dennis C. Daley, *Dual Diagnosis Workbook: Recovery Strategies for Addiction and Mental Health Problems*. Session 24, "Changing My Thinking," pp. 127–131. Independence, Missouri: Herald House/Independence Press, 1994.

- J. Howell and M. Thase, *Beating the Blues: Recovery from Depression*. Section 7, "Changing Thoughts and Beliefs," pp. 23–24. Skokie, Illinois: Gerald T. Rogers Productions (1-800-227-9100).

- Dennis C. Daley, *Overcoming Negative Thinking*. Section 4, "Countering Negative Thinking," and Section 5, "How to Change Negative Beliefs," pp. 21–26. Minneapolis, Minnesota: Johnson Institute, 1991 (1-800-231-5165).

PE GROUP #39
Developing Spirituality
In Dual Recovery

Objectives

- Acquaint client with the spiritual aspect of recovery.
- Identify ways in which spirituality can aid recovery as well as positive self-change.
- Clients understand the "we" aspect versus the "I" aspect of recovery.
- Identify Steps of the AA, NA, CA, or DRA program that address spirituality issues.

Methods/Major Points

- Use a lecture/discussion format. Write major points on a chalkboard or flip chart for reinforcement.
- State that recovery is multidimensional. One very important aspect is spirituality. Ask clients to define spirituality as they see it and what it means to their recovery.
- Discuss "values and meaning" as an aspect of spirituality. Ask clients to state what relationships, activities, or values give them the most meaning and purpose in their life at this time.
- Discuss recovery as a "we" process involving relationships with other people and a "Higher Power." State that while most choose to use God as their Higher Power, some find other sources of a Higher Power. The important issue is not to rely solely on oneself in recovery and to reach out for help and support from others.
- State that as recovery progresses, serving others is one way of developing spirituality. Helping others is the basis of Step 12. However, this is only done after a substantial period of recovery.
- State that many of the 12 Steps address spirituality, especially Steps 2, 3, 4, 5, 6, 7, 11, and 12.
- Ask clients to identify one area related to their spirituality that they would like to work on developing.
- Discuss strategies to develop spirituality. Add additional ones to supplement the ideas generated by clients. Strategies may include the following:

  1. Rely on God or a Higher Power for strength, guidance, purpose in life, and understanding.
  2. Participate in religious services and other religious activities.
  3. Make praying a regular part of the day or join a prayer group.
  4. Attend a religious retreat or spend time at a monastery or other spiritual place to get in touch with spiritual beliefs.
  5. Meditate.
  6. Read the Bible or other spiritual and inspirational guides to seek knowledge, guidance, and motivation.

146

7. Discuss spirituality issues in therapy sessions or with an AA/NA sponsor.

8. Focus on the 12-Step program, especially Steps 2, 3, 4, 5, 6, 7, 11, and 12.

9. Seek spiritual advice from a priest, minister, rabbi, or other spiritual person.

10. Focus on the greater good of society and contributions that can be made to make the world a better place.

11. Be of service to others (e.g., through volunteer work).

12. Show love and compassion in daily life in interactions with other people.

13. Be kind and forgiving to others.

14. Accept one's own weaknesses and limitations and be kind to oneself and tolerant of shortcomings and mistakes.

15. Stop hurtful behaviors toward others and make amends as needed.

Supporting Materials

- Dennis C. Daley, *Dual Diagnosis Workbook: Recovery Strategies for Addiction and Mental Health Problems*. Session 25, "Developing My Spirituality," pp. 132–134. Independence, Missouri: Herald House/Independence Press, 1994.
- Terence T. Gorski, *Keeping the Balance: A Psychospiritual Model of Growth and Development*. Independence, Missouri: Herald House/Independence Press, 1993.
- List of the 12 Steps.

PE GROUP #40
Using a Daily Plan in Recovery From Dual Disorders

Objectives

- Clients understand the importance of having a "daily plan" to follow in recovery.
- Clients learn how to develop a daily plan.
- Connect the idea of a daily recovery plan with the notion of a "daily inventory" stressed in 12-Step programs; one of the similarities is for clients to take a "proactive" approach in planning daily activities related to recovery or other areas of functioning.

Methods/Major Points

- Use a lecture/discussion format. Write major points on a chalkboard or flip chart for reinforcement.
- Ask clients why they think it is important to have a daily plan to follow in their ongoing recovery. Add examples as needed to cover these benefits:

    1. Helps keep one focused
    2. Keeps one busy
    3. Helps one achieve goals
    4. Helps one spot problems early

- Discuss the possible negative consequences of not having or following a recovery plan on a daily basis. Add examples as needed to cover the following potential problems:

    1. Problems are not identified or addressed promptly
    2. Boredom and hopelessness are more likely
    3. One can lose focus on recovery
    4. The risk of relapse increases

- Ask clients what specific activities should be included in this daily plan. Emphasize the following possible activities (all won't be used every day):

    1. Support group meetings (AA, NA, CA, DRA, Mental Health groups)
    2. Discussion with sponsor or other members of support network
    3. Treatment sessions (individual, family, group)
    4. Taking medication

148

5. Working the 12-Step program

6. Using other "tools" of the program (slogans, literature, etc.)

7. Praying or using a Higher Power

8. Positive self-talk (to manage cravings, cope with anger or depression, etc.)

9. Challenging negative self-talk

10. Self-reflection (daily inventory, completion of daily written journal entry, etc.)

11. Reading recovery literature

12. Taking a few minutes at the beginning of each day to review the day's recovery plan

13. Taking a few minutes at the end of the day to review how things went, and to identify problems early that need attention

- Optional: Discuss using a daily schedule and/or weekly schedule to help in this process. Provide samples of plans and blank planning schedules for clients to practice.

Supporting Materials

- Dennis C. Daley, *Dual Diagnosis Workbook: Recovery Strategies for Addiction and Mental Health Problems.* Session 26, "My Daily Plan For Recovery," pp. 136–138. Independence, Missouri: Herald House/Independence Press, 1994.
- Blank copy of daily schedule.
- Blank copy of weekly schedule.

PE GROUP #41
Financial Issues in Dual Recovery

Objectives

- Identify financial problems caused or worsened by alcohol or other drug use or psychiatric illness.
- Identify strategies to reduce debt.
- Identify strategies to handle money more effectively.

Methods/Major Points

- Use a lecture/discussion format. Write major points on a chalkboard or flip chart for reinforcement.
- State that financial problems are associated with dual disorders. Although either disorder can cause money problems, more commonly alcohol/drug addiction does the most financial damage. Financial problems can cause frustration, anger, and hopelessness.
- Ask clients to give examples of financial problems caused or worsened by their disorders. Include financial effects on the family as well as clients. Some of the more common money problems include:

    1. loss of income due to money spent on alcohol or drugs (Using paycheck or government checks to purchase drugs or support alcohol habit is very common.);

    2. loss of income due to inability to get or keep a job;

    3. inability to pay bills on time (rent, utilities, food, etc.) or meet basic needs for food and shelter;

    4. inability to provide adequately for children or family (food, clothing, shelter, etc.);

    5. accumulating a large "drug debt," which can also put a person's safety in danger due to retaliation by drug pushers who don't get their money; and

    6. getting deeply in debt due to above problems, or due to borrowing money at high rates of interest from loan sharks or financial institutions.

- Help clients identify strategies to address their financial problems and to help them manage their money more effectively. Money management strategies to review include:

    1. Reading books and magazines to learn new ways of managing money

    2. Keeping track of money

    3. Developing and following a budget to live within financial means

    4. Regularly reviewing progress and changing budget plan as needed

5. Reducing debts on loans and credit cards

6. Avoiding loan sharks and high interest loans

7. Shopping more effectively to stretch money

8. Figuring out the "little ways" to save money here and there (all of which can add up to substantial savings)

9. When to use a financial counselor or seek special help for money problems

- Some clients may have no income at all. The goal with them is to find ways of financial support until they get back on their feet. This support may have to come initially from the government in the form of welfare. These clients may also benefit from information on food banks and other sources of help (e.g., help with utility payments).

Supporting Materials

- *Dual Diagnosis Workbook: Recovery Strategies for Addiction and Mental Health Problems.* Session 28, "Financial Recovery," and Session 29, "Strategies for Handling Money and Debt," pp. 143–148. Independence, Missouri: Herald House/Independence Press, 1994.

- List of local resources and phone numbers (welfare office, food banks, etc.).

PE GROUP #42
Relapse Warning Signs

Objectives

- Clients learn that warning signs typically precede a psychiatric relapse or a drug/alcohol relapse.
- Introduce the idea that relapse is a *process* as well as an event.
- Review *common warning signs* associated with psychiatric relapse and drug/alcohol relapse.
- Review *subtle warning signs* that may be unique to each individual.
- Clients learn that once they notice warning signs, they need to have a plan to manage these warning signs *before* things get worse. The earlier they catch the warning signs the better.
- For those clients who have had one or more episodes of relapse, they learn to use this as a *learning experience* to help their future recovery.

Methods/Major Points

- Use a lecture/discussion format. Write the major points on a chalkboard or flip chart for reinforcement.
- Ask the group to define relapse from both the psychiatric and drug/alcohol points of view. Then give the following definitions:

    1. Psychiatric relapse refers to return of symptoms after a period of remission or a significant worsening of persistent symptoms.

    2. Addiction relapse refers to the process of returning to alcohol or drug use.

- Ask group members who have relapsed to either disorder to give examples of relapse warning signs from past experiences. Add additional examples as needed and state that warning signs will fall in one or more of the following categories:

    1. Changes in thinking ("I don't need recovery, it's not worth the effort)

    2. Changes in mood (significant increase in anger, boredom, or depression)

    3. Changes in health habits or daily routines (not taking care of personal hygiene or drastic change in daily habits)

    4. Changes in behavior (stopping or cutting down on treatment or support group meetings)

- For addiction relapse, emphasize it seldom "comes out of the blue." Discuss the context of relapses (who, where, when) and help clients see that it may be days, weeks, or longer between the emergence of warning signs and subsequent alcohol or drug use.
- Emphasize the importance of catching relapse warning signs early. The earlier clients intervene, the less likely major damage or suffering will occur.

- Ask the group to come up with coping strategies for several select warning signs. Their specific examples should fall in the following broad categories:

  1. Cognitive

  2. Behavioral

  3. Interpersonal

- Use this information to emphasize the importance of being aware of warning signs and having a plan to cope with them.

- Tie in the concept of getting support from others to cope with warning signs (e.g., AA/NA friends and sponsors, counselor, friends, family, etc.).

Supporting Materials

- Dennis C. Daley, *Dual Diagnosis Workbook: Recovery Strategies for Addiction and Mental Health Problems*. Session 31, "Relapse Warning Signs," pp. 153–158. Independence, Missouri: Herald House/Independence Press, 1994.
- Videotapes from Gerald T. Rogers Productions (1-800-227-9100): *Living Sober: Coping with Relapse Warning Signs and High Risk Situations* (1994). *Staying Sober, Keeping Straight* (1988).

PE GROUP #43
Coping with High-Risk Relapse Factors

Objectives

- Clients learn that certain factors increase the chances of relapse, both in relation to psychiatric relapse and alcohol/drug relapse. Label these as high-risk relapse factors.

- Clients learn that relapse risk factors fall into different categories, and it is usually a combination of factors, rather than just one, that contribute to relapse.

- Clients learn that it isn't just the high-risk factors (or causes of relapse) but how they think about these (beliefs) and cope (coping skills) with them that determine whether or not a relapse will occur.

- Identify strategies to manage high-risk relapse factors.

Methods/Major Points

- Use a lecture/discussion format. Write the major points on a chalkboard or flip chart for reinforcement.

- State that there are a number of external and internal factors that increase clients' vulnerability to relapse. These are referred to as "high-risk factors."

- Ask group members to identify what they consider to be their high-risk relapse factors, both in relation to their psychiatric disorder and their chemical dependency. Each client should identify at least one high-risk factor.

- Review the major categories of causes of relapse, giving some examples from each category.

  1. Intrapersonal or internal factors (thoughts, feelings)

  2. External factors (relationships, support system, etc.)

  3. Lifestyle factors (health habits, structure, etc.)

- Stress the importance of having a plan to deal with potential high-risk factors. The general idea is to:

  1. identify (anticipate) high-risk factors;

  2. develop coping strategies to manage relapse risk factors;

  3. implement coping strategies in daily recovery; and

  4. change strategies that don't work and try new ones.

- Reinforce the importance of making a commitment to long-term recovery using both professional counseling and self-help programs such as AA, NA, DRA, and mental health support groups. This provides an ongoing mechanism to cope with high-risk factors.

154

- Stress that some people are more vulnerable to relapse than others, based on the history and severity of their illnesses. For example:

  1. A client with several episodes of recurrent depression is more vulnerable to a relapse than a first-timer in treatment.

  2. A client with a long history of addiction and multiple attempts at recovery is more vulnerable to relapse than a first timer.

Supporting Materials

- Dennis C. Daley, *Relapse Prevention Workbook: For Recovering Alcoholics and Drug Dependent Persons*. Sections 3 and 4, "Identifying High Risk Situations," and "Strategies to Handle High Risk Situations," pp. 4–9. Holmes Beach, Florida: Learning Publications, 1986 (1-800-222-1525).
- Dennis C. Daley and L. Roth, *When Symptoms Return: Relapse and Psychiatric Illness*. Section 3, "Causes of Relapse," pp. 9–12. Holmes Beach, Florida: Learning Publications, 1992 (1-800-222-1525).
- Videotapes from Gerald T. Rogers Productions (1-800-227-9100): *Living Sober: Coping with Relapse Warning Signs and High Risk Situations* (1994); *Staying Sober, Keeping Straight* (1988).

PE GROUP #44
Coping with Emergencies and Setbacks

Objectives

- Clients learn the importance of being prepared to handle setback emergencies (i.e., a return to chemical use or a return or worsening of psychiatric symptoms).
- Identify potential benefits of continued involvement in treatment and recovery.
- Clients learn that failure to comply with ongoing treatment increases the chances of a chemical use or psychiatric relapse.

Methods/Major Points

- Use a lecture/discussion format. Write the major points on a chalkboard or flip chart for reinforcement.
- State that studies and our clinical experience show that clients who comply with treatment do better than those who do not. Failure to comply with treatment often contributes to relapse.
- Stress the importance of taking medications even after symptoms are under control.

  1. Medication can keep symptoms under control.
  2. Medications reduce the likelihood of a psychiatric relapse.

- Ask clients who have failed to comply with treatment in the past, and those who did, to state how this affected their addiction and psychiatric disorder.
- Ask clients to identify the potential benefits of complying with treatment.
- State that many people relapse, so it helps to be prepared should this occur. Relapse can occur even if clients comply with treatment. However, it is less likely if treatment is complied with. Ask clients to identify the potential benefits of preparing ahead of time for a setback or relapse.
- Ask clients what they could do if they felt their treatment plan wasn't working (i.e., instead of dropping out of treatment):

  1. talk to their treatment team;
  2. talk to a sponsor; or
  3. try to figure out why the plan isn't working.

- Ask clients to identify steps they could take if they relapsed to chemical use.

  1. stop using and get rid of booze or drugs;
  2. ask for help from a sponsor or other AA, NA, CA friends;
  3. ask for help from the treatment team; and
  4. seek detoxification if physical addiction has reoccurred.

- Ask clients to identify steps to take if psychiatric symptoms returned or worsened. Emphasize the importance of talking with the treatment team.
- Review the following ideas about setbacks and emergencies:

  1. Preparing ahead of time allows clients to catch setbacks early that may help prevent a full-blown relapse.

  2. Clients can ask for help with setbacks or emergencies from counselors, other professionals, and sponsors.

  3. When possible, the family should be involved.

  4. Clients who decompensate psychiatrically and become suicidal, homicidal, or unable to care for themselves will probably need to be hospitalized. If they refuse, which is often due to poor judgment, an involuntary commitment may be needed.

  5. Clients who get readdicted physically and can't stop alcohol or drug use will need to be detoxified under medical supervision.

Supporting Materials

- Dennis C. Daley, *Dual Diagnosis Workbook: Recovery Strategies for Addiction and Mental Health Problems.* Session 30, "The Importance of Follow-up after Rehabilitation or Hospital-based Treatment," pp. 150–152; Session 31, "Relapse Warning Signs," pp. 153–158. Independence, Missouri: Herald House/Independence Press, 1994.
- Dennis C. Daley, *Relapse Prevention Workbook*: Sections 9 and 10, "Building a Long-Term Sobriety Plan" and "Emergency Sobriety Card," pp. 17–19. Holmes Beach, Florida: Learning Publications, 1986 (1-800-222-1525).
- Videotape: *Staying Sober, Keeping Straight.* Gerald T. Rogers Productions (1-800-227-9100).

References

1. L.N. Robins and D.A. Regier, eds., *Psychiatric Disorders in America: The Epidemiologic Catchment Area Study* (New York: The Free Press, 1991).

2. D. Daley, H. Moss, and F. Campbell, *Dual Disorders: Counseling Clients with Chemical Dependency and Mental Illness*, 2nd ed. (Center City, Minnesota: Hazelden, 1993).

3. D. O'Connell, ed., *Managing the Dually Diagnosed Patient* (New York: Haworth Press, 1991).

4. D. Daley and M. Raskin, eds., *Treating the Chemically Dependent and Their Families* (Newbury Park, California: Sage Publications, 1991).

5. J.H. Lowinson, P. Ruiz, and R.B. Millman, *A Comprehensive Textbook of Substance Abuse*, 2nd ed. (Baltimore, Maryland: Williams and Wilkins, 1992).

6. G. Woody and D. Mercer, *Individual Drug Counseling*, manual developed for NIDA-sponsored clinical trial (Philadelphia: University of Pennsylvania, 1993).

7. D. Mercer, G. Carpenter, D. Daley, et al., *Group Drug Counseling*, manual developed for NIDA-sponsored clinical trial (Philadelphia: University of Pennsylvania, 1993).

8. A. Beck, *Cognitive Therapy and the Emotional Disorders* (New York: International Universities Press, 1976).

9. H. Kaplan and B. Sadock, eds., *Comprehensive Textbook of Psychiatry, Volumes 1 & 2*, 5th ed. (Baltimore, Maryland: Williams and Wilkins, 1989).

10. F. Goodwin and K. Jamison, *Manic Depressive Illness* (New York: Oxford University Press, 1990).

11. M.E. Thase, "Relapse and Recurrence in Unipolar Major Depression: Short-term and Long-term Approaches," *Journal of Clinical Psychiatry* 51, no. 6 (1990): 51–57.

12. A.T. Beck and A. Freeman, *Cognitive Therapy of Personality Disorders* (New York: The Guilford Press, 1990).

13. E. Frank, D.J. Kupfer, J.M. Perel, et al., "Three-year Outcomes for Maintenance Therapies in Recurrent Depression," *Archives of General Psychiatry* 47 (1989): 1093–1099.

14. G.A. Marlatt and J.R. Gordon, *Relapse Prevention* (New York: The Guilford Press, 1985).

15. D. Daley, *Relapse Prevention: Treatment Alternatives and Counseling Aids* (Bradenton, Florida: Human Services Institute, 1988).

16. R.P. Liberman, *Social and Independent Living Skills Symptom Management Module—Patient Workbook* (Los Angeles: UCLA Department of Psychiatry, 1988).

17. R.P. Liberman, W.J. DeRisi, and K.T. Mueser, *Social Skills Training for Psychiatric Patients* (New York: Pergamon Press, 1989).

18. M.M. Linehan, *Skills Training Manual for Treating Borderline Personality Disorder* (New York: The Guilford Press, 1993).

19. T. Gorski and M. Miller, *Staying Sober: A Guide for Relapse Prevention* (Independence, Missouri: Herald House/Independence Press, 1986).

20. T. Gorski, *How to Start Relapse Prevention Support Groups* (Independence, Missouri: Herald House/Independence Press, 1989).

21. C.M. Anderson, D.J. Reiss, and G.E. Hogarty, *Schizophrenia and the Family: A Practitioner's Guide to Psychoeducation and Management* (New York: The Guilford Press, 1986).

22. A.B. Hatfield, *Family Education in Mental Illness* (New York: The Guilford Press, 1990).

23. D. Daley, K. Bowler, and H. Cahalane, "Approaches to Patient and Family Education in Affective Illness," *Journal of Patient Education and Counseling* 19 (1992): 163–174.

24. D. Daley and J. Miller, *Taking Control: A Family Guide to Chemical Dependency* (Holmes Beach, Florida: Learning Publications, 1993).

25. G.I. Keitner, *Depression and Families: Impact and Treatment* (Washington, D.C.: American Psychiatric Press, 1990).

26. J. Clarkin, G. Haas, and I. Glick, *Affective Disorders and the Family* (New York: The Guilford Press, 1988).

27. A.B. Hatfield and H.P. Lefley, *Families of the Mentally Ill: Coping and Adaptation* (New York: The Guilford Press, 1987).

28. D. Daley, I. Salloum, and A. Jones-Barlock, "Integrating a Dual Disorders Program in an Acute Care Psychiatric Hospital," *Journal of Psychosocial Rehabilitation* 15, no. 2 (1991): 45–56.

29. K. Minkoff and R.E. Drake, *Dual Diagnosis of Major Mental Illness and Substance Disorder* (San Francisco: Jossey-Bass, 1991).

30. E. Kaufman, "The Psychotheraphy of Dually Diagnosed Patients," *Journal of Substance Abuse Treatment* 6 (1989): 9–18.

31. E.P. Nace, "Alcoholism and Other Psychiatric Disorders." In *The Treatment of Alcoholism* (New York: Brunner/Mazell, 1987).

32. *Alcoholics Anonymous* "Big Book" (New York: AA World Services, 1976).

33. *Narcotics Anonymous* "Basic Text" (Sun Valley, California: NA World Services Office, 1983).

34. *The Dual Disorders Recovery Book* (Center City, Minnesota: Hazelden, 1993).

35. R.E. Meyer, ed., *Psychopathology and Addictive Disorders* (New York: The Guilford Press, 1986).

36. D. Daley, *Chemical Dependency and Mental Illness: A Resource Guide for Dual Disorders* (Holmes Beach, Florida: Learning Publications, 1992).

37. M.A. Schuckit, "The Relationship between Alcohol Problems, Substance Abuse and Psychiatric Syndromes." In *DSM-IV Source Book, Volume I* (Washington, D.C.: American Psychiatric Press), 45–66.

38. R.C. Cloninger, "Neurogenetic Adaptive Mechanisms in Alcholism," *Science* (1987): 410–416.

39. A. McLellan, L. Luborsky, G. Woody, C. O'Brien, and K. Druley, "Predicting Response to Alcohol and Drug Abuse Treatments: Role of Psychiatric Severity," *Archives of General Psychiatry* 40 (1983): 620–625.

40. R. Catalano, M. Howard, J. Hawkins, and E. Wells, "Relapse in the Addictions: Rates, Determinants, and Promising Prevention Strategies." In *1988 Surgeon General's Report on Health Consequences of Smoking* (Washington, D.C.: Office of Smoking and Health, U.S. Government Printing Office, 1988).

41. J.O. Prochaska, J.C. Norcross, and C.C. DiClemente, *Changing for Good* (New York: William Morrow and Company, 1994).

42. S. Zimberg, "Principles of Alcoholism Psychotherapy." In S. Zimberg, J. Wallace, and S. Blume, eds., *Practical Approaches to Alcoholism Psychotheraphy*, 2nd ed. (New York: Plenum Publishing Corporation, 1985).

43. W.E. McAuliffe and J. Albert, *Clean Start: An Outpatient Program for Initiating Cocaine Recovery* (New York: The Guilford Press, 1992).

44. R.A. Rawson, J.L. Obert, M.J. McCann, D.P. Smith, and W. Ling, "Neurobehavioral Treatment for Cocaine Dependency," *Journal of Psychoactive Drugs* 22, no. 2 (1990): 159–171.

45. The "Group Adherence Scale" was adapted from one developed by Delinda Mercer, Gloria Carpenter, and Dennis Daley; the "Individual Scale" was adapted from one developed by Delinda Mercer and George Woody.

46. L. Gerstley, et al., "Ability to Form an Alliance with the Therapist: A Possible Marker of Prognosis for Patients with Antisocial Personality Disorder," *American Journal of Psychiatry* 146, no. 4 (1989): 508–512.

47. G.E. Woody, et al., "Sociopathy and Psychotherapy Outcome," *Archives of General Psychiatry* 42 (1985): 1081–1086.

48. *Diagnostic and Statistical Manual of Mental Disorders (DSM-IV)*, 4th ed. (Washington, D.C.: American Psychiatric Press).

49. A. McLellan, et al., *Guide to the Addiction Severity Index*, DHHS Publ. No. (ADM) 85-1419 (Rockville, Maryland: National Institute on Drug Abuse, 1985).

50. R. Tarter and A.M. Hegedus, "The Drug Use Screening Inventory: Its Application in the Evaluation and Treatment of Alcohol and Drug Abuse," *Alcohol Health and Research World* (1991).

51. H.A. Skinner, "The Drug Abuse Screening Test," *Addictive Behaviors* 7 (1982): 363–371.

52. M.L. Selzer, "The Michigan Alcoholism Screening Test: The Quest for a New Diagnostic Instrument," *American Journal of Psychiatry* 127 (1971): 1653–1658.

53. J.T. Sullivan, K. Sykora, J. Schneiderman, C.A. Narango, and E.M. Sellers, "Assessment of Alcohol Withdrawal: The Revised Clinical Institute Withdrawal Assessment of Alcohol Withdrawal (CIWA-Ar)," *British Journal of Addiction* 84 (1989): 1353–1357.

54. J.L. Horn, K.W. Wanberg, and F.M. Foster, *The Alcohol Use Inventory* (Baltimore, Maryland: Psych Systems, 1983).

55. J.B.W. Williams, M. Gibbon, M.B. First, R.L. Spitzer, M. Davies, J. Borus, M.J. Howes, J. Kane, H.G. Pope, B. Rounsaville, and H. Wittchen, "The Structured Clinical Interview for DSM-III-R (SCID) II: Multisite Test-retest Reliability," *Archives of General Psychiatry* (in press).

56. R.L. Spitzer, J.B.W. Williams, M. Gibbon, and M.B. First, *Structured Clinical Interview for DSM-III-R — Patient Edition (with Psychotic Screen)* (Washington, D.C.: American Psychiatric Press, 1990).

57. A.T. Beck, N. Epstein, and G. Brown, "An Inventory for Measuring Clinical Anxiety," *Journal of Consulting and Clinical Psychology* 56 (1988): 893–897.

58. A.T. Beck, R.A. Steer, and M.G. Garbin, "Psychometric Properties of the Beck Depression Inventory: Twenty-five Years Later," *Clinical Psychology Review* 8 (1988): 77–100.

59. M. Hamilton, "The Assessment of Anxiety States by Rating," *British Journal of Medical Psychology* 32 (1959): 50–55.

60. M. Hamilton, "A Rating Scale for Depression," *Journal of Neurological and Neurosurgical Psychiatry* 23 (1960): 56–62.

61. P. Bech, T.G. Bolwig, P. Kramp, and O.J. Rafaelsen, "The Bech-Rafaelsen Mania Scale and the Hamilton Depression Scale," *Acta Psychiatrica Scandinavica* 59 (1979): 420–430.

62. J. Carroll, *Substance Abuse Problem Checklist* (Eagleville, Pennsylvania: Eagleville Hospital, 1983).

63. W.R. Miller and S. Rollnick, *Motivational Interviewing: Preparing People to Change Addictive Behavior* (New York: The Guilford Press, 1991).

64. K.B. Carey and M.P. Carey, "Enhancing the Treatment Attendance of Mentally Ill Chemical Abusers," *J Behav Ther & Exp Psychiat* 21, no. 3 (1990): 205–209.

65. A. Chen, "Noncompliance in Community Psychiatry: A Review of Clinical Interventions," *Hospital and Community Psychiatry* 42, no. 3 (1991): 282–287.

66. P.J. Carpenter, G.R. Morrow, A.C. Del Gaudio, and B.A. Ritzler, "Who Keeps the First Outpatient Appointment?" *American Journal of Psychiatry* 138 (1981): 102–105.

67. D.A. Krulee and R.E. Hales, "Compliance with Psychiatric Referrals from a General Hospital Psychiatry Outpatient Clinic," *General Hospital Psychiatry* 10 (1988): 339–345.

68. R. Tessler and J.H. Mason, "Continuity of Care in the Delivery of Mental Health Services," *American Journal of Psychiatry* 136 (1979): 1297–1301.

69. D.L. Bogin, S.S. Anish, H.A. Taub, et al., "The Effects of a Referral Coordinator on Compliance with Psychiatric Discharge Plans," *Hospital and Community Psychiatry* 35 (1984): 702–706.

70. E.B. Fink and C.L. Heckerman, "Treatment Adherence after Brief Hospitalization," *Comprehensive Psychiatry* 22 (1981): 379–385.

71. W. Kruse, "Patient Compliance with Drug Treatment—New Perspectives on an Old Problem," *The Clinical Investigator* 70 (1992): 163–166.

72. D.L. Goldman and R.M. Post, "The Puzzle of Noncompliance in the Manic Patient," *Bulletin of the Menninger Clinic* 55 (1991): 248–253.

73. V. Agosti, E. Nunes, J.W. Stewart, and F.M. Quitkin, "Patient Factors Related to Early Attrition from an Outpatient Cocaine Research Clinic: A Preliminary Report," *The International Journal of the Addictions* 26, no. 3 (1991): 327–334.

74. R.M. Kadden and I.J. Mauriello, "Enhancing Participation in Substance Abuse Treatment Using an Incentive System," *Journal of Substance Abuse Treatment* 8 (1991): 133–134.

75. N.J. Hochstadt and J. Trybula, Jr., "Reducing Missed Initial Appointments in a Community Mental Health Center," *Journal of Community Psychology* 8 (1980): 261–265.

76. W.M. Addenbrooke and N.H. Rathod, "Relationship between Waiting Time and Retention in Treatment amongst Substance Abusers," *Drug and Alcohol Dependence* 26 (1990): 255–264.

77. P.H. Kleinman, S.Y. Kang, D.S. Lipton, G.E. Woody, J. Kemp, and R.B. Millman, "Retention of Cocaine Abusers in Outpatient Psychotherapy," *American Journal of Drug and Alcohol Abuse* 18, no. 1 (1992): 29–43.

78. M.S. Ridgely and M.L. Willenbring, "Application of Case Management to Drug Abuse Treatment: Overview of Models and Research Issues." In *Progress and Issues in Case Management (NIDA Research Monograph 127)*, edited by R.S. Ashery (Rockville, Maryland: National Institute on Drug Abuse, 1992), 12–33.

Appendices

1. **Additional Suggested Readings**

2. **Suggested Client and Family Educational Materials**

3. **Educational Films**

4. **Self-Help Programs**

1. Additional Suggested Readings

Alter, A. *Summary of the Research Exchange Meeting of Young Adult Chronic Patients*. Rockville, Maryland: Alcohol, Drug Abuse, and Mental Health Administration, 1990.

Alterman, A., ed. *Substance Abuse and Psychopathology*. New York: Plenum Press, 1985.

Ananth, J., S. Vandewater, M. Kamal, et al. "Missed Diagnosis of Substance Abuse in Psychiatric Patients," *Hospital and Community Psychiatry* 40, no. 3 (1989): 297–299.

Anderson, C.M., and S. Stewart. *Mastering Resistance: A Practical Guide to Family Therapy*. New York: The Guilford Press, 1983.

Attia, P.R. "Dual Diagnosis: Definition and Treatment," *Alcoholism Treatment Quarterly* 5, nos. 3/4 (1988): 53–63.

Beck, A.T., G. Emery, and R.L. Greenberg. *Anxiety Disorders and Phobias*. New York: Basic Books, 1985.

Beck, A.T., F.D. Wright, C.F. Newman, and B.S. Liese. *Cognitive Therapy of Substance Abuse*. New York: The Guilford Press, 1993.

Bedi, A., and J. Halikas. "Alcoholism and Affective Disorder," *Alcoholism: Clinical and Experimental Research* 9, no. 2 (1985): 133–134.

Bergman, H.C., and M. Harris. "Substance Abuse among Young Chronic Patients," *Psychosocial Rehabilitation Journal* 9, no. 1 (1985): 49–54.

Bisbee, C. *Educating Patients and Families about Mental Illness: A Practical Guide*. Gaithersburg, Maryland: Aspen Publishers, 1991.

Blume, S.B. "Dual Diagnosis: Psychoactive Substance Abuse and the Personality Disorders," *Journal of Psychoactive Drugs* 21, no. 2 (1989): 139–144.

Brown, T.A., and D.H. Barlow. "Panic Disorder and Panic Disorder with Agoraphobia." In *Principles and Practice of Relapse Prevention*, edited by P.H. Wilson, 191–212. New York: The Guilford Press, 1992.

Brown, U.B., M.S. Ridgely, B. Pepper, et al. "The Dual Crisis: Mental Illness and Substance Abuse," *American Psychologist* 44, no. 3 (1989): 565–569.

Cadoret, R., T. O'Gorman, E. Troughton, and E. Heywood. "Alcoholism and Antisocial Personality," *Archives of General Psychiatry* 42 (1985): 161–167.

Caragonne, P., and B. Emery. *Mental Illness and Substance Abuse: The Dually Diagnosed Client*. Rockville, Maryland: National Council of Community Mental Health Centers, 1987.

Carey, K.B. "Emerging Treatment Guidelines for Mentally Ill Chemical Abusers," *Hospital and Community Psychiatry* 40, no. 4 (1989): 341–349.

Chiauzzi, E. *Preventing Relapse in the Addictions: A Biopsychosocial Approach*. New York: Pergamon Press. 1991.

Cohen, J., and S.J. Levy. *The Mentally Ill Chemical Abuser: Whose Client?* New York: Lexington Books, 1992.

"Co-morbidity of Addictive and Psychiatric Disorders," special edition of the *Journal of Addictive Diseases* 12, no. 3 (1993), edited by N. Miller and B. Stimmel.

Cooper, G., and C. Kent. "Special Needs of Particular Populations: Dual Disorders." In *Alcohol and Drug Problems: A Practical Guide for Counselors*, edited by B.A. Howard and L. Lightfoot. Toronto: Addiction Research Foundation, 1990.

Cornelius, J.R., I.M. Salloum, M.D. Cornelius, J.M. Perel, M.E. Thase, J.G. Ehler, and J.J. Mann. "Fluoxetine Trial in Suicidal Depressed Alcoholics," *Psychopharmacology Bulletin* 29 (1993): 195–199.

Cornelius, J.R., I.M. Salloum, J. Mezzich, M.D. Cornelius, H. Fabrega, J.G. Ehler, R.F. Ulrich, M.E. Thase, and J.J. Mann. "Disproportionate Suicidality in Patients Presenting with Comorbid Major Depression and Alcoholism," *American Journal of Psychiatry* (in press).

Craske, M.G., T.A. Brown, and D.H. Barlow. "Behavioral Treatment of Panic: A Two-year Follow-up," *Behavior Therapy* 22 (1991): 289–304.

Daley, D. *Chemical Dependency and Mental Illness: A Resource Guide for Dual Disorders*. Holmes Beach, Florida: Learning Publications, 1992.

_____. *Living Sober: An Interactive Video Recovery Program—Counseling Manual*. Skokie, Illinois: Gerald T. Rogers Productions, 1994.

DeLeon, G. "Psychopathology and Substance Abuse: What Is Being Learned in Therapeutic Communities?" *Journal of Psychoactive Drugs* 21, no. 2 (1989): 177–188.

Dilsauer, S. "The Pathophysiologies of Substance Abuse and Affective Disorders: An Integrative Model," *Journal of Clinical Psychopharmacology* 7 (1987): 1–10.

Donovan, D.M., and G.A. Marlatt. *Assessment of Addictive Behaviors*. New York: The Guilford Press, 1988.

Dorus, W., J. Kennedy, R. Gibbons, and S. Ravis. "Symptoms and Diagnosis of Depression in Alcoholics," *Alcoholism: Clinical and Experimental Research* 11, no. 2 (1987): 150–154.

Drake, R., and M. Wallach. "Substance Abuse among the Chronic Mentally Ill," *Hospital and Community Psychiatry* 40, no. 10 (1989): 1041–1049.

El-Guebaly, N. "Substance Abuse and Mental Dsorders: The Dual Diagnoses Concept," *Canadian Journal of Psychiatry* 35, no. 3 (1990): 261–267.

Ellis, A., J.F. McInerney, R. DiGiuseppe, and R.J. Yeager. *Rational-Emotive Therapy with Alcoholics and Substance Abusers*. New York: Pergamon Press, 1988.

Emmelkamp, P.M.G., T.K. Bouman, and A. Scholing. *Anxiety, Phobias and Obsessive-Compulsive Disorders: A Clinical Guide*. London: Wiley, 1991.

Emmelkamp, P.M.G., J. Kloek, and E. Blaauw. "Obsessive-Compulsive Disorders." In *Principles and Practice of Relapse Prevention*, edited by P.H. Wilson, 213–234. New York: The Guilford Press, 1992.

Estroff, T.W., C.A. Dackis, M.S. Gold, et al. "Drug Abuse and Bipolar Disorder," *International Journal of Psychiatric Medicine* 15 (1985): 37–40.

Evans, K., and J.M. Sullivan. *Dual Diagnosis: Counseling the Mentally Ill Substance Abuser*. New York: The Guilford Press, 1990.

Frances, R.J., and S.I. Miller, eds. *Clinical Textbook of Addictive Disorders*. New York: The Guilford Press, 1991.

Galanter, M., R. Casteneda, and J. Ferman. "Substance Abuse among General Psychiatric Patients: Place of Presentation, Diagnosis and Treatment," *American Journal of Drug and Alcohol Abuse* 14, no. 2 (1988): 211–235.

Gottheil, E., A.T. McClellan, and K.A. Druley, eds. *Substance Abuse in Psychiatric Illness*. Elmsford, New York: Pergamon, 1980.

Heinrichs, D.W., B.P. Cohen, and T. Carpenter. "Early Insight and the Management of Schizophrenic Decompensation," *Journal of Nervous and Mental Disease* 173, no. 3 (1985): 133–138.

Hellerstein, D.J., and B. Meehan. "Outpatient Group Therapy for Schizophrenic Substance Abusers," *American Journal of Psychiatry* 144 (1987): 1337–1339.

Hollon, S.D., M.D. Evans, and R.J. DeRubeis. "Cognitive Mediation of Relapse Prevention Following Treatment for Depression: Implications for Differential Risk." In *Contemporary Approaches to Depression*, edited by R.E. Ingram, 117–136. New York: Plenum Press, 1990.

Howland, R.H., and M.E. Thase. "A Comprehensive Review of Cyclothymic Disorder. *Journal of Nervous Mental Disorder* 181 (1993): 485–493.

Jackson, H., and J. Edwards. "Social Networks and Social Support in Schizophrenia: Correlates and Assessment." In *Schizophrenia: An Overview and Practical Handbook*, edited by D.J. Kavanagh, 275–292. London: Chapman & Hall, 1992.

Johnson, S.L., S. Monroe, A. Simons, and M.E. Thase. "Clinical Characteristics Associated with Interpersonal Depression: Symptoms, Course and Treatment Response," *Journal of Affective Disorders* 31 (1994): 97–109.

Kadden, R., K. Carroll, D. Donovan, N. Cooney, P. Monti, D. Abrams, M. Litt, and R. Hester. *Cognitive-Behavioral Coping Skills Therapy Manual: A Clinical Research Guide for Therapists Treating Individuals with Alcohol Abuse and Dependence*. Rockville, Maryland: National Institute on Alcohol Abuse and Alcoholism, 1992.

Kavanagh, D.J. "Schizophrenia." In P.H. Wilson, ed., *Principles and Practice of Relapse Prevention*, 157–190. New York: The Guilford Press, 1992.

Kavanagh, D.J., ed. *Schizophrenia: An Overview and Practical Handbook*. London: Chapman & Hall, 1992.

Kofoed, L., and A. Keys. "Using Group Therapy to Persuade Dual-diagnosis Patients to Seek Substance Abuse Treatment," *Hospital and Community Psychiatry* 39, no. 11 (1988): 1209–1211.

Kosten, T.R., and H.D. Kleber, eds. *Clinician's Guide to Cocaine Addiction: Theory, Research and Treatment*. New York: The Guilford Press, 1992.

Kosten, T.R., and H.D. Kleber, "Differential Diagnosis of Psychiatric Comorbidity in Substance Abusers," *Journal of Substance Abuse Treatment* 5 (1988): 201–206.

Kranzler, H.R., and N.R. Liebowitz. "Anxiety and Depression in Substance Abuse, *Medical Clinics of North America* 72, no. 4 (1988): 867–885.

Kupfer, D.J., E. Frank, J.M. Perel, C. Cornes, A.G. Mallinger, M.E. Thase, A.B. McEachran, and V. Grochocinski. "Five-year Outcome for Maintenance Therapies in Recurrent Depression,". *Archives of General Psychiatry* 49 (1992): 769–773.

Laws, R.D., ed. *Relapse Prevention with Sex Offenders*. New York: The Guilford Press, 1989.

Layden, M.A., C.F. Newman, A. Freeman, and S.B. Morse. *Cognitive Therapy of Borderline Personality Disorder*. Boston: Allyn and Bacon, 1993.

Leverich, G.S., R.M. Post, and A.S. Rosoff. "Factors Associated with Relapse during Maintenance Treatment of Affective Disorders," *International Clinical Psycho-pharmacology* 5 (1990): 135–156.

Lewinsohn, P.M., D.O. Antonuccio, J.S. Breckenridge, and L. Teri. *The Coping with Depression Course: A Psychoeducational Intervention for Unipolar Depression*. Eugene, Oregon: Castalia Publishing Company, 1984.

Liberman, J.A., J.M. Kane, S. Sarantakos, et al. "Prediction of Relapse in Schizophrenia," *Archives of General Psychiatry* 44 (1987): 597–603.

Linehan, M.M. *Cognitive-Behavioral Treatment of Borderline Personality Disorder*. New York: The Guilford Press, 1993.

McAuliffe, W.E., and J. Albert. *Clean Start: An Outpatient Program for Initiating Cocaine Recovery*. New York: The Guilford Press, 1992.

Meek, P.S., H.W. Clark, and V.L. Solana. "Neurocognitive Impairment: The Unrecognized Component of Dual Diagnosis in Substance Abuse Treatment," *Journal of Psychoactive Drugs* 21, no. 2 (1989): 153–161.

Menicucci, L.D., L. Wermuth, and J. Sorensen. "Treatment Providers' Assessment of Dual-prognosis Patients: Diagnosis, Treatment, Referral, and Family Involvement," *International Journal of the Addictions* 23, no. 6 (1988): 617–622.

Merikangas, K., J. Leckman, B. Prusoff, et al. "Familial Transmission of Depression and Alcoholism," *Archives of General Psychiatry* 42 (1985): 367–372.

Miklowitz, D.J., M.J. Goldstein, K.H. Nuechterlein, et al. "Family Factors and the Course of Bipolar Affective Disorder," *Archives of General Psychiatry* 45 (1988): 225–231.

Miller, N.S., ed. *Treating Co-existing Psychiatric and Addictive Disorders*. Center City, Minnesota: Hazelden, 1994.

Mirin, S., and R. Weiss. "Psychopathology in Substance Abusers: Diagnosis and Treatment," *American Journal of Drug and Alcohol Abuse* 14, no. 2 (1988).

Monroe, S.M., A.D. Simons, and M.E. Thase. "Onset of Depression and Time to Treatment Entry: The Roles of Life Stress," *Journal of Consulting and Clinical Psychology* 59 (1991): 566–573.

Monti, P.M., D.B. Abrams, R.M. Kadden, and N.L. Cooney. *Treating Alcohol Dependence: A Coping Skills Training Guide*. New York: The Guilford Press, 1989.

Moss, H.B., J.K. Yao, and G.L. Panzak. "Serotonergic Responsivity and Behavioral Dimensions in Antisocial Personality Disorder with Substance Abuse," *Society of Biological Psychiatry* 28 (1990): 325–338.

Nace, E., J. Saxon, and N. Shore. "Borderline Personality Disorder and Alcoholism Treatment: A One-year Follow-up Study," *Journal of Studies on Alcohol* 47, no. 3 (1986): 195–200.

National Institute of Drug Abuse. "Dual Diagnosis: Drug Abuse and Psychiatric Illness." In *Drug Abuse and Drug Abuse Research. Third Report to Congress*, 61–83. Rockville, Maryland: National Institute of Drug Abuse, 1990.

Nowinski, J., S. Baker, and K. Carroll. *Twelve Step Facilitation Therapy Manual: A Clinical Research Guide for Therapists Treating Individuals with Alcohol Abuse and Dependence*. Rockville, Maryland: National Institute on Alcohol Abuse and Alcoholism, 1992.

Osher, F., and L. Kofoed. "Treatment of Patients with Psychiatric and Psychoactive Substance Abuse Disorders," *Hospital and Community Psychiatry* 40, no. 10 (1989): 1025–1030.

Pepper, B., and H. Ryglewicz. *The Young Adult Chronic Patient*. San Francisco: Jossey-Bass, 1982.

Regier, D., et al. "Co-morbidity of Mental Disorders with Alcohol and Other Drug Abuse: Results from the Epidemiologic Catchment Area Study," *Journal of the American Medical Association* 264, no. 19 (1990): 2511–2518.

Rounsaville, B., Z. Dolinsky, T. Babor, and R. Meyer. "Psychopathology as a Predictor of Treatment Outcome in Alcoholics," *Archives of General Psychiatry* 44, no. 6 (1987): 505–513.

Rounsaville, B.J., F.H. Gawin, and H.D. Kleber. "Interpersonal Psychotherapy Adapted for Ambulatory Cocaine Abusers," *American Journal of Drug and Alcohol Abuse* 11 (1985): 171–191.

Safer, D.J. "Substance Abuse by Young Adult Chronic Patients," *Hospital and Community Psychiatry* 38, no. 5 (1987): 511–514.

Salloum, I.M., H.B. Moss, and D.C. Daley. "Substance Abuse and Schizophrenia: Impediments to Optimal Care," *The American Journal of Drug and Alcohol Abuse* 17, no. 3 (1991): 321–336.

Schneier, F.R., and S.G. Siris. "A Review of Psychoactive Substance Use and Abuse in Schizophrenia," *Journal of Nervous and Mental Disease* 175, no. 11 (1987): 641–652.

Schofield, M.A. "The Contribution of Problem Drinking to the Level of Psychiatric Morbidity in the General Hospital," *British Journal of Psychiatry* 155 (1989): 229–232.

Schuckit, M. "Genetic and Clinical Implications of Alcoholism and Affective Disorder," *American Journal of Psychiatry* 143, no. 2 (1986): 140–147.

Schuckit, M., and M.G. Montiero. "Alcoholism, Anxiety and Depression," *British Journal of Psychiatry* 88 (1988): 1373–1380.

Solomon, J., S. Zimberg, and E. Shollar, eds. *Dual Diagnosis: Evaluation, Treatment, Training, and Program Development*. New York: Plenum Medical Book Company, 1993.

Stuart, S., and M.E. Thase. "Inpatient Applications of Cognitive Behavior Therapy: A Review of Recent Developments," *Journal of Psychotherapy Practice and Research* (in press).

Thase, M.E. "Inpatient Cognitive Behavior Therapy of Depression." In *Less Time to Do More: Psychotherapy on the Short-Term Inpatient Unit*, E. Leibenluft, A. Tasma, and S.A. Green, eds, 111–140. Washington, D.C.: American Psychiatric Press, 1993.

_____. "Maintenance Treatments of Recurrent Affective Disorders. In H.L. Freeman and D.J. Kupfer, eds., *Current Opinion in Psychiatry* 6 (1993): 16–21.

_____. "Relapse and Recurrence in Unipolar Major Depression: Short-term and Long-term Approaches," *Journal of Clinical Psychiatry* 51, no. 6: 51–57.

Thase, M.E., K. Bowler, and T. Harden. "Cognitive Behavior Therapy of Endogenous Depression: Part 2: Preliminary Findings in 16 Unmedicated Patients," *Behavior Therapy* 22 (1991): 469–477.

Thase, M.E., M. Hersen, and B.A. Edelstein, eds. *Handbook of Outpatient Treatment of Adults*. New York: Plenum Press, 1990.

Thase, M.E., C.F. Reynolds III, E. Frank, A.D. Simons, G.D. Garamoni, J. McGeary, T. Harden, A.L. Fasiczka, and J.F. Cahalane. "Response to Cognitive Behavior Therapy in Chronic Depression," *Journal of Psychotherapy Practice and Research* 3 (1994): 204–214.

Thase, M.E., A.J. Rush, S. Kaspar, and C. Nermeroff. "Tricyclics and Newer Antidepressant Medication: Treatment Options for Treatment Resistant Depressions," *Depression* (in press).

Thase, M.E., and A.D. Simons. "The Applied Use of Psychotherapy in the Study of the Psychobiology of Depression," *Journal of Psychotherapy Practice and Research* 1 (1992): 72–80.

Thase, M.E., A.D. Simons, J. Cahalane, and J. McGeary. "Cognitive Behavior Therapy of Endogenous Depression: Part 1: An Outpatient Clinical Replication Series," *Behavior Therapy* 22 (1991): 457–467.

Thase, M.E., A.D. Simons, J. Cahalane, J. McGeary, and T. Harden. "Severity of Depression and Response to Cognitive Behavior Therapy," *American Journal of Psychiatry* 148 (1991): 784–789.

Thase, M.E., A.D. Simons, J. McGeary, J.F. Cahalane, C. Hughes, T. Harden, and E. Friedman. "Relapse after Cognitive Behavior Therapy of Depression: Potential Implications for Longer Courses of Treatment?" *American Journal of Psychiatry*, 149 (1992): 1046–1052.

Thase, M.E., and J.H. Wright. "Cognitive Behavior Therapy Manual for Depressed Inpatients: A Treatment Protocol Outline," *Behavior Therapy* 22 (1991): 579–595.

Vaillant, G. "Natural History of Male Alcoholism V: Is Alcoholism the Cart or the Horse to Sociopathy?" *British Journal of Addiction* 78 (1983): 317–326.

Vannicelli, M. *Removing the Roadblocks: Group Psychotherapy with Substance Abusers and Family Members.* New York: The Guilford Press, 1992.

Wallace, B.C. *Crack Cocaine: A Practical Treatment Approach for the Chemically Dependent.* New York: Brunner/Mazel, 1991.

Washton, A.M. *Cocaine Addiction: Treatment, Recovery, and Relapse Prevention.* New York: W.W. Norton & Company, 1989.

Westermeyer, J. "Treatment for Psychoactive Substance Use Disorder in Special Populations: Issues in Strategic Planning." *Advances in Alcohol and Substance Abuse* 8, nos. 3/4 (1990): 1–8.

Wilson, P.H., ed. *Principles and Practice of Relapse Prevention.* New York: The Guilford Press, 1992.

Woody, G.E., A.T. McLellan, and C.P. O'Brien. "Research on Psychopathology and Addiction: Treatment Implications," *Drug and Alcohol Dependence* 25 (1990): 121–123.

Wright, J.H., and M.E. Thase. "Cognitive and Biological Therapies: A Synthesis," *Psychiatric Annals* 22 (1992): 451–458.

Wright, J.H., M.E. Thase, A.T. Beck, and J.W. Ludgate, eds. *Cognitive Therapy with Inpatients.* New York: The Guilford Press, 1992.

Yalom, I.D. *Inpatient Group Psychotherapy.* New York: Basic Books, 1983.

_____. *Theory and Practice of Group Psychotherapy*, 3rd ed. New York: Basic Books, 1984.

Zackon, F., W.E. McAuliffe, and J.M.N. Ch'ien. *Recovery Training and Self-Help: Relapse Prevention and Aftercare for Drug Addicts.* Rockville, Maryland: National Institute on Drug Abuse, 1993.

Zweben, J.E. "Recovery-oriented Psychotherapy: Facilitating the Use of 12-Step Programs," *Journal of Psychoactive Drugs* 19, no. 2 (1987): 243–252.

Zweben, J.E., and D.E. Smith. "Considerations in Using Psychotropic Medication with Dual Diagnosis Patients in Recovery," *Journal of Psychoactive Drugs* 21, no. 2 (1989): 221–228.

2. Suggested Client and Family Educational Materials

Alcoholics Anonymous ("Big Book"). New York: AA World Services, Inc., 1976.

Agras, S. *Facing Fears, Phobias and Anxiety*. New York: Freeman, 1985.

Brown, K.D. *The Learn Program for Weight Control*. Philadelphia: University of Pennsylvania, 1989.

Bourne, E. *The Anxiety and Phobia Workbook*. Oakland, California: New Harbinger Publications, 1990.

Burns, D. *The Feeling Good Workbook*. New York: William Morrow, 1990.

Club, G.A. *Coping with Panic*. Belmont, California: Brooks/Cole, 1990.

Daley, D. *Coping with Anger Workbook*. Skokie, Illinois: Gerald T. Rogers Productions, 1991.

_____. *Coping with Feelings Workbook*. Holmes Beach, Florida: Learning Publications, 1994.

_____. *Dual Diagnosis Workbook: Recovery Strategies for Addiction and Mental Health Problems*. Independence, Missouri: Herald House/Independence Press, 1994.

_____. *Family Recovery Workbook: For Families Affected by Chemical Dependency*. Bradenton, Florida: Human Services Institute, 1987.

_____. *Improving Communication and Relationships*. Holmes Beach, Florida: Learning Publications, scheduled release in 1995.

_____. *Living Sober: An Interactive Video Recovery Program—Client Workbook*. Skokie, Illinois: Gerald T. Rogers Productions, 1994.

_____. *Overcoming Negative Thinking*. Minneapolis, Minnesota: Johnson Institute, 1991.

_____. *Preventing Relapse*. Center City, Minnesota: Hazelden, 1993.

_____. *Relapse: A Guide for Successful Recovery*. Bradenton, Florida: Human Services Institute, 1987.

_____. *Relapse Prevention Workbook: For Recovering Alcoholics and Drug Dependent Persons*. Holmes Beach, Florida: Learning Publications, 1986.

_____. *Surviving Addiction Workbook: Practical Tips on Developing a Recovery Plan*. Holmes Beach, Florida: Learning Publications, 1990.

_____. *Working Through Denial: The Key to Recovery*. Minneapolis, Minnesota: Johnson Institute, 1990.

Daley, D., and L. Bennett. *Recovery from Psychiatric Illness: A Guide to Psychiatric Hospitalization*. Holmes Beach, Florida: Learning Publications, 1992.

Daley, D., and F. Campbell. *Coping with Dual Disorders: Chemical Dependency and Mental Illness*, 2nd ed. Center City, Minnesota: Hazelden, 1993.

Daley, D., and K. Montrose. *Understanding Schizophrenia and Addiction*. Center City, Minnesota: Hazelden, 1993.

Daley, D., and L. Roth. *When Symptoms Return: Relapse and Psychiatric Illness*. Holmes Beach, Florida: Learning Publications, 1992.

Daley, D., and J. Sinberg. *A Family Guide to Coping with Dual Disorders*. Center City, Minnesota: Hazelden, scheduled for release in 1995.

Daley, D., and C. Sproule. *Adolescent Relapse Prevention Workbook*. Holmes Beach, Florida: Learning Publications, 1991.

Ellis, A. *How to Stubbornly Refuse to Make Yourself Miserable About Anything*. Secaucus, New Jersey: Lyle Stuart, 1988.

Evans, K., and M. Sullivan. *Step Study Counseling for the Dually Diagnosed*. Center City, Minnesota: Hazelden, 1991.

Glanz, L. *Overcoming Anxiety and Worry*. Skokie, Illinois: Gerald T. Rogers Productions, 1991.

Gondolf, E.W., and D.M. Russell. *Man to Man: A Guide for Men in Abusive Relationships*. Bradenton, Florida: Human Services Institute, 1987.

Goodwin, D.W. *Anxiety*. New York: Oxford University Press, 1986.

Gorski, T. *Passages Through Recovery: An Action Plan for Preventing Relapse*. Center City, Minnesota: Hazelden, 1989.

_____. *Keeping the Balance: A Psychospiritual Model of Growth and Development*. Independence, Missouri: Herald House/Independence Press, 1993.

_____. *Relapse Prevention Therapy with Chemically Dependent Criminal Offenders—Part 3*. Independence, Missouri: Herald House/Independence Press, 1993.

_____. *Relapse Prevention Workbook for the Criminal Offender*. Independence, Missouri: Herald House/ Independence Press, 1993.

_____. *The Staying Sober Workbook: A Serious Solution for the Problem of Relapse*. Independence, Missouri: Herald House/Independence Press, 1989 (revised, 1992).

_____. *Understanding the Twelve Steps: A Guide for Counselors, Therapists, and Recovering People*. Independence, Missouri: Herald House/Independence Press, 1989.

Gorski, T., and M. Miller. *Staying Sober: A Guide for Relapse Prevention*. Independence, Missouri: Herald House/ Independence Press, 1986.

Haskett, R., and D. Daley. *Understanding Bipolar Disorder and Addiction*. Center City, Minnesota: Hazelden, 1994.

Howell, J., and M.E. Thase. *Beating the Blues: Recovery from Depression*. Skokie, Illinois: Gerald T. Rogers Productions, 1991.

Jeffers, S. *Feel the Fear and Do It Anyway*. New York: Fawcett Columbine, 1987.

Kreisman, J., and H. Straus. *I Hate You—Don't Leave Me: Understanding the Borderline Personality*. New York: Avon Books, 1989.

Lerner, H. *The Dance of Anger*. New York: Harper and Row, 1985.

Lewinsohn, P., et al. *Control Your Depression*. New York: Prentice Hall, 1986.

Liberman, R. *Social and Independent Living Skills: Symptom Management Module*. Los Angeles: UCLA Department of Psychiatry, 1988.

Markway, B.G., et al. *Dying of Embarrassment: Help for Social Anxiety and Phobia*. Oakland, California: New Harbinger, 1992.

Martorano, J.T. *Beyond Negative Thinking: Breaking the Cycle of Depressing and Anxious Thoughts*. New York: Insight Books, 1989.

Miller, M., T. Gorski, and D. Miller. *Learning to Live Again: A Guide for Recovery from Chemical Dependency*, updated and revised ed. Independence, Missouri: Herald House/Independence Press, 1992.

Mondimore, F.M. *Depression: The Mood Disease*, revised ed. Baltimore, Maryland: The Johns Hopkins University Press, 1993.

Narcotics Anonymous ("Basic Text"). Sun Valley, California: NA World Services, 1993.

Papolos, D., and J. Papolos. *Overcoming Depression*. New York: Harper and Row, 1987.

Rapoport, J.L. *The Boy Who Couldn't Stop Washing: The Experience and Treatment of Obsessive-Compulsive Disorder*. New York: New American Library, 1989.

Read, L., and D. Daley. *Getting High and Doing Time: What's the Connection?* Laurel, Maryland: American Correctional Association, 1990.

Rosellini, G., and M. Worden. *Of Course You're Anxious*. Center City, Minnesota: Hazelden, 1988.

_____. *Here Comes the Sun*. Center City, Minnesota: Hazelden, 1988.

Salloum, I., and D. Daley. *Understanding Major Anxiety Disorders and Addiction*. Center City, Minnesota: Hazelden, 1994.

Seagrave, A., and F. Covington. *Free from Fears: New Help for Anxiety, Panic and Agoraphobia*. New York: Poseidon Press, 1994.

Sheehan, D. *The Anxiety Disease*. New York: Charles Scribner and Sons, 1984.

Tauris, C. *Anger: The Misunderstood Emotion*, 2nd ed. New York: Simon and Schuster, 1989.

Thase, M., and D. Daley. *Understanding Depression and Addiction*. Center City, Minnesota: Hazelden, 1994.

The Dual Recovery Book. Center City, Minnesota: Hazelden, 1993.

Weekes, C. *More Help for Your Nerves.* New York: Bantam Books, 1984.

Weiss, R., and D. Daley. *Understanding Personality Problems and Addiction.* Center City, Minnesota: Hazelden, 1994.

Worden, M. *Depression and Recovery from Chemical Dependency.* Center City, Minnesota: Hazelden, 1990.

3. Educational Films

Staying Sober, Keeping Straight. Skokie, Illinois: Gerald T. Rogers Productions, 1988.

Together: Families in Recovery. Skokie, Illinois: Gerald T. Rogers Productions, 1989.

Double Trouble: Recovery from Chemical Dependency and Mental Illness, Part I—Mood and Anxiety. Skokie, Illinois: Gerald T. Rogers Productions, 1990.

Double Trouble: Recovery from Chemical Dependency and Mental Illness, Part II—Personality Disorders. Skokie, Illinois: Gerald T. Rogers Productions, 1990.

Why Are You So Angry? Skokie, Illinois: Gerald T. Rogers Productions, 1991.

Relapse Prevention: Mentor Series Training Videotapes. Skokie, Illinois: Gerald T. Rogers Productions, 1992.

Living Sober: Resisting Social Pressures to Use Chemicals. Skokie, Illinois: Gerald T. Rogers Productions, 1992.

Living Sober: Coping with Cravings and Thoughts of Using. Skokie, Illinois: Gerald T. Rogers Productions, 1994.

Living Sober: Managing Anger in Recovery. Skokie, Illinois: Gerald T. Rogers Productions, 1994.

Living Sober: Managing Feelings of Boredom and Emptiness. Skokie, Illinois: Gerald T. Rogers Productions, 1994.

Living Sober: Coping with Family and Interpersonal Conflict. Skokie, Illinois: Gerald T. Rogers Productions, 1994.

Living Sober: Building a Recovery Network and Sponsorship. Skokie, Illinois: Gerald T. Rogers Productions, 1994.

Living Sober: Coping with Relapse Warning Signs. Skokie, Illinois: Gerald T. Rogers Productions.

Living Sober: Recovering from Crack/Cocaine Addiction. Skokie, Illinois: Gerald T. Rogers Productions, 1994.

Preventing Relapse. Center City, Minnesota: Hazelden, 1994.

Understanding Anxiety Disorders and Addiction. Center City, Minnesota: Hazelden, 1994.

Understanding Depression and Addiction. Center City, Minnesota: Hazelden, 1994.

4. Self-Help Programs

Dual Recovery Anonymous, Central Service Office, P.O. Box 8170, Prairie Village, KS 66208 (phone: 913/676-7226). A self-help organization for those with dual disorders (Twelve-Step format).

Double Trouble. Some AA chapters have special meetings for recovering individuals who have alcohol and mental health problems combined. These groups have a variety of names, depending on the area of the country.

Emotional Health Anonymous, 2420 Gabriel Boulevard, Rosemead, CA 91880 (phone: 818/240-3215). A Twelve-Step program for people with psychiatric problems.

Grow, Inc., 2403 West Springfield, Champaign, IL 61821 (phone: 217/352-6989). A self-help program for people with psychiatric problems.

Mentally Ill Recovering Alcoholics (MIRA), P.O. Box 8335, Rolling Meadows, IL 60008.